OPTIONS TRADING STRATEGIES

Best Beginners Guide On Learn How To Create Your
Passive Income On Forex, Futures, Swing Trading &
Stock Investing Quickly. Master Money Management
Psychology & Start Your First Online Business

ROBERT SMITH

© Copyright 2020 - All rights reserved.

Table Of Contents

Introduction

I f you have spent any time looking at the world of investing, you may have heard about options at one point or another. They are sometimes going to seem pretty overwhelming to think about, but if you know a few key points that come with them, options can be pretty easy to understand. Options can be seen as another class of assets, just like mutual funds, ETFs, bonds, and stocks. Options can be a powerful tool because they are going to do some wonders when it comes to enhancing your portfolio. Based on the situation, you will find some sort of options contract that can provide you with an adequate alternative. In turbulent times, options are a great means of protecting your portfolio against sharp and unexpected declines.

In addition to protecting some of your assets, options are sometimes used to generate a recurring income. And some investors will choose to use these in a more speculative purpose, such as wagering on the direction that a stock will take. Just like with any of the other choices that you make with investing, options will involve some risks and you must fully understand these and know how to avoid them as much as possible. This is why any time you want to start trading options with a broker, there is going to be some kind of disclaimer like the following to help you know about the risk with options: Only invest in risk capital. Options are going to belong to a larger group of securities that are known as derivatives. This is a word that many investors are going to associate with excessive risk-taking. In the past, Warren Buffett has even referred to these derivatives as a weapon of mass destruction when it comes to the stock market.

While there is some truth to this assertion, particularly when it comes to the irresponsible use of derivatives, the fact is that most derivatives are a good way for smaller investors to make some tidy profits. However, it is important to be aware that a derivative is a financial instrument that is based on the value on what is known as an "underlying asset". This means that the valuation of the contact will depend on the valuation of the asset that it is tied to. It should also be noted that you never actually own the asset when you take out an option until that option is exercised. You never actually sell the asset until the option goes through.

If you already know how these options are going to work, and the right way to use them, you are going to have a huge advantage when trading in the market. Options are also nice because they will ensure the odds are put in your favor. If using options as a form of speculation doesn't seem to fit with the risks that you want to take or your trading choices, then you can also do options without any speculating. Even if you do decide to never work with options, it is important to understand how companies you invest in will use them. Some companies may use this to hedge their foreign exchange risk or give employees some stock ownership as well. And most of the multi-national corporations today are going to work with options in some form or another, and even as an individual investor you can use it to invest in many different securities.

There are two main types of options. The first is called a "call option". This option receives this name as it gives the bearer the right to buy. However, it does not constitute an obligation. What this means is that, if for whatever reason, the bearer chooses not to exercise their option, this is not penalized in any way. If the contract is exercised, then the bearer must go through with the purchase of the underlying security at the price agreed. This price is referred to as the "strike price".

The second type of option is called a "put option". This sort of option means that the bearer has the right to sell the underlying asset, but the contract itself does not represent an obligation to go through with the deal. This means that if the seller chooses to change their mind, they are free to do so as long as the provisions in the contract are met.

One way that you can think about a call option is like having a down payment for a future purpose. For instance, a potential homeowner sees that in an area of their town, there is a new development that is about to go up. This homeowner may decide that they want the right to purchase one of the homes in that area in the future, but they only want to be able to exercise that right once there are certain developments built around that area. Maybe they want to make sure that some schools are built there first or some other great amenities before they choose to purchase. These kinds of circumstances would then be able to affect the decision of the homeowner to purchase the home in that area. The potential homebuyer would benefit from the option of buying or not depending on whether the promised amenities show up or not and they can agree to purchase the home at a predetermined level.

In this example, the potential buyer could benefit greatly especially if and when prices for that property, or that sector, go up. Let's assume that both the seller and buyer agree at a sale price of $100,000. The buyer gets a call option for this price for two months. At the maturity of the option, the buy has the right to purchase the property. Besides, the seller cannot sell the home to anyone else during that period even if the market value of the property goes up and other buyers offer more money. The seller can negotiate but cannot make a deal unless the option is exercised or declined.

If after the two months the option is exercised, the buyer goes through with the deal paying the $100,000 strike price. The buyer can make a great deal of money if the valuation of the property increases. For instance, if the valuation goes up to $125,000, the buyer can then turn around and resell at the higher price. The option also protects the buyer in case the price of the property falls. For instance, if they valuation falls from $100,000 to $80,000, the buyer has the option to decline. This can save the buyer from losing on the deal. The seller, of course, misses out on the sale and would have to figure out what to do with the property moving forward.

This is why options are seen as insurance policies. They can protect investors from purchasing assets which may suddenly decline in value, or lock in the price of an asset which is expected to go up at some point. If the buyer, or seller, decide not to go through with the option, they only lose the underwriting fee that goes along with the option itself. When you think about it, it's a small price to pay considering the potential losses that you could face especially in a volatile market.

What if, instead of a home, your asset was a stock or another investment vehicle. This is what is going to happen when we look at options trading and doing a put option. If you have an S&P 500 index portfolio, you have a choice to purchase one of these put options. An investor may choose to do this if they fear that a bear market is going to happen soon, and they refuse to lose more than ten percent of their long position in the portfolio. If the S&P 500 is currently trading at $2500, the trader can purchase a put option that provides them with the right to sell that index at $2250 at any point during a certain expiration date, such as within a few years. Then, if in six months or twelve months or another period in that two years, the market ends up crashing by twenty percent, which is 500 points on the index, the trader has made 250 points by being able to still sell the index at $2250 when it is trading at $2000. This is a great option to help the trader only lose ten percent on their portfolio, even if the market goes down by twenty percent, or even more.

Of course, acquiring an option is not free. There is an implicit cost that comes with all options. This cost is a fee that is charged by the underwriter of the contract. This fee is charged to cover the expenses that the underwriter incurs when drafting the option.

The underwriter is an independent third party that looks to establish a neutral playing ground. None of the stakeholders in the contract may underwrite it (the buy or seller) as this would be deemed a conflict of interest. In this regard, the individual who takes out the option, regardless of its nature, must cover this fee. The fee is called a premium and may be subject to negotiation. For instance, both parties may agree to split the cost of the premium in case the option is exercised. Otherwise, the bearer would have to cover the cost.

CHAPTER 1:

Options Trading: The Basics

Options trading refers to a contractual agreement between two parties in which the buying party gets the right to trade a security at a predetermined price and a predetermined date. The right, however, is not obligatory. The right is given to the buyer by the seller through the payment of premiums. Options trading involves trading with stocks and securities for profit and also keen to avoid incurring losses. In options trading, the buyer is also referred to as the taker in the contract. The seller is usually referred to as the writer.

Types of Options Trading

Two types of options trading grant two different rights. The first one is termed as call options. They give the buyer rights to purchase the asset that is underlying the contract on a later date depending at a predetermined price. This right is, however, not obligatory and is usually based on the discretion of the taker or the contract and his understanding of the market performance in the course of the life of the contract. The life of the contract refers to the period before the contract expires. The price of buying the contract is termed as the exercise price. Sometimes it is also referred to as the strike price.

An example of call options is if Santos Limited has a contract available with shares on security that has the last sale price of $6.00. If the contract has a three-month expiry period, the taker then has the option of offering the shares for a call of $6.00. One can buy 100 token offerings of securities at the said call price per share at the time of choice for the taker in the course of the life of the contract. The taker is also required to pay premiums to the writer of the contract for the option.

To fully own the call rights, one has to exercise it based on the predetermined dates that are specified in the agreement.

On the hand, the writer of the contract must ensure that the shares that are purchased are delivered. In the above example, the writer has to deliver 100 security token offerings as long as the taker of the contract has exercised the option. However, the writer sustains reception of option premium during the life of the contract regardless of Put whether or not the taker exercises the option.

The other form of options is the put options. These are designed to grant the taker rights of selling the underlying assets for a price that has been predetermined by the contract. The rights to sell have to be exercised in the course of the life of the contract. Just like the call options, the taker of the contract is not compelled to exercise the right. In this case, the buyer only provides the shares required in the agreement if the put right is exercised.

An example of a put option is when a contract by the writer has a predetermined $6.00 put token offering for a predetermined period of three months. The taker has a put option of selling 100 security token offerings as shares at the said price of $6.00 per share. This sell right has to be exercised in eth active life of the contract by the date of expiry of the agreement.

As with the call option, the taker still has to pay premiums to the writer for the contract and the trade to be valid. The right is only valid when it is exercised with the course of the life of the contract. Outside of it, the right is forfeited regardless of whether or not value was created out of the contract. This means that the taker of the contract has to be keen on market performance and judge well whether or not to invoke the sell rights and when. Sometimes, a taker will opt not to exercise the right of sale of shares as the contract expiry dies out.

The exercise style is usually dependent on the system used. Two systems are usually used: the American style and the European style. The

European style usually compels the taker to exercise the right in the contract only on the expiry date. The American style is more flexible and allows the exercise of the right any time before the date of expiry of the agreement.

Components of an Option Contract

There are various standardized components of option contracting that enable ease in engaging in options trading. These components characterize the mechanics of how options trading binds the parties involved and demonstrates the ay profits can be generated if the market forces are favorable. Among the components of options trading are:

- Underlying securities

- Contract size

- Expiry day

- Exercise prices

Underlying securities

Options that are traded on the market only apply to certain assets. These assets are then referred to as underlying securities. The word shares can be replaced with the word shares in certain instances. Some companies provide the asset against which the option operators list options. ASX is one operator in the options trading market has played a key role in the listing of underlying securities.

The term classes of options refer to the listing of puts and calls as options of the same assets. As an example, is when puts and calls are applied to a lease corporation's shares. This does not put in regard the contract terms in terms of the predetermined price or duration of expiry of the call and put contracts. An operator of options trading usually provides the list of the available classes for the benefit of investors.

Contract Size

On the ASX platform of options trading, the market standardizes the size of the option contract at 100 underlying securities. One option contract, therefore, corresponds to 100 underlying shares. The changes that can happen only come when reorganization happens on the initial outlay of the underlying share or the capital therein. Index options usually fix the value of the contract at a certain stipulated dollar rate.

Expiry day

Options are constrained by time and have a life span. There are predetermined expiry deadlines that the platform operator sets which have to be respected. These deadlines are usually rigid, and once they are out the rights under a contract in a particular class of unexercised options are then forfeited. Usually, the last day of the life span of a contract is the summative trading date. For shares that have their expiry coming by June of 2020, the options over them have their last trading day on a Thursday that comes before the last Friday that happens to be in the month. Those that expire beyond June 2020, expiry is on the third Thursday that happens to be in the month. For index options. Expiries come on the concurrent third Thursday of the same month of writing the option. However, these dates can be readjusted by the options platform operator as and when there is a reason for such action.

In recent years, platform operators have introduced more short-term options for some underlying. Some are weekly, while others are on a fortnightly basis. These have the corresponding weekly or fortnightly expiries. When the life span of options run out, the operators then create new deadlines. However, all classes of options have their expiries subject to quarters of the financial calendar.

Exercise Prices

These are the buying price or the price of selling the assets or underlying securities. These prices are also called strike prices. They are usually predetermined in the option contract and have to be met if one has to exercise the rights in an option. Essentially, they are called exercise because the parties are now invoking the rights that are stipulated in an option either to buy or sell. The exercise of the option is, therefore, subject to the price stipulations.

The platform operator usually predetermines the prices. Various prices can be listed as available on the market for the same expiry of a certain class of options. Usually, prices depend on the value of the underlying share value. If the value of the underlying prices increases, the exercise prices also increase commensurately. The need to offer a range of prices for the same option contract is to suit the market conveniences of buyers of the contracts. The buyer can better match their expectations of the pricing of the underlying shares given the position of their option contract. The exercise prices can also be varied in the course of an active contract when market dynamics dictate that such a move has to be made.

Premium

This is the value of the option that is usually expressed as a price that has to be paid by the option taker. Of the five features of options trading, this is the only one that is not determined by the platform operator. Usually, the premium prices are stated in cents corresponding to the value per share. To get the premium that has to be paid, for an option that is of relatively standard size, a formula is set. One has to take the premium price that has been stipulated on the option contract and multiply by the sum of the shares that a contract has.

For example, when the cost of a premium has been quoted as 16 cents. This has to be multiplied by the standard shares for every option, which is 100. This brings the payable premium for the option to $16.00. For an index option, there is another formula that offers a modality of calculating the premium. Index options have a standard multiplier index of $10. The quoted premium is therefore multiplied by this index multiplier to result to the total payable premium.

Having exercised the rights under an option contract, there are guidelines about being eligible to vote and to earn dividends from the shares. The buyer in the case of a call option does not gain express rights to earn dividends on the shares. One has to wait until the exercised right of purchase is affected by the transfer of the shares. The same applies to vote rights. Usually, shares represent a voice in the company invested in. however; the voting rights also wait or the transfer of the shares to the buyer.

Similarly, the seller or writer in the put option does not expressly acquire the right to vote and earn dividends. One waits until the underlying assets, securities, or shares are transferred. This helps to create a structure of transfer of shareholding and transfer of the same. Any disputes about the expired contract have to be resolved, and proper registration of buying and selling be done for the holding trading the shares or asset.

Adjustments to Option Contracts

There is a general effort to ensure that option contracts are entered in under conditions that are standardized to the greatest extent possible. However, some market forces may upset the set optimum conditions and specifications. This may call or the making of some adjustments to ensure the preservation of the value attached to the positions of the various options contracts that have been entered into by various takers and writers.

CHAPTER 2:

Best Options Strategies

Bull Call Spreads

One of the biggest benefits of trading options is that you don't need to be worried about the current market situation since your trades are designed to profit in all markets. At the very least, you will have a strategy, no matter what the market is doing. The bull call spread, also called the long call spread, is a strategy for a moderate to strong bullish market.

In this scenario, you're quite certain that the stock is going to increase in value over the medium term but you're a bit uncertain about the volatility it is showing. You see, there is a dose of uncertainty with every directional position and you are compensated for this with higher rewards. Options strategies take this uncertainty away but cap your maximum reward. Thus, if you're extremely certain that a stock is going to go upwards for sure, buying a long call is probably the best strategy. After all, if you know a stock is going to increase in value, why would you place a cap on your profits by writing a call at a higher strike price?

Such situations are extremely rare; however, and this is where the bull call spread comes into action.

How it Works

With the bull call spread, you will be buying a long call which is either in the money or close to the money and offsetting this price by writing an out of the money call. If the stock goes past the higher strike price, your long call is in profit but your overall profit is capped to the level of the higher strike price.

If the stock goes below your long call, you have the premium of the higher strike price call to offset your loss, which is simply the premium you paid for the long call. Remember, you're not buying any stock in this strategy so there is no loss on the stock itself.

Let's continue to use AAPL as an example of this. As of this writing, AAPL is trading at $173.3. The closest at the money call option in the near month is the $170 and $175 which is trading at $6.95 and $4.10 respectively. Now, you could choose either of these strike prices. Remember, you're moderately bullish on the stock but are not sure how high it will go. Given these conditions, let's purchase the 175 call for $4.10.

Now, we need to find a suitable strike price to write a call at. This is a tricky balancing act. Write a call too far away and you won't receive enough of a premium. Write one too close, and you're not giving your trade enough breathing room. This is why it's essential to keep your time horizon on this trade as short as you can afford to. Ideally, your options will have some time value left on them but not too much time so as to bring price uncertainty into them.

The time decay is evident in the current month option prices. The $190 option is selling for $0.37 which is a pittance really. However, let's stick with the current month for now. So, what do our risk and reward look like?

Maximum risk= Premium paid for long call- Premium received for short call= 4.1-0.37= 3.73.

Maximum reward= Strike price of short call- Strike price of long call- cost paid for entering the trade= 190-175-3.73= 11.27

Thus, our reward/risk on this 3X. Just to clarify, the prices quoted for an option contract are on a per share basis. Since every contract contains a hundred shares, you should multiply the price by a hundred to get the full price of the contract.

So, to enter this position, or to purchase a single contract, we will need to spend $373 and if the price hits our higher strike price of $190 then we'll clear $1127 on the trade. These numbers are with the near month options, of course. Let's look at how the numbers change by taking the far month into consideration.

Price of far month $175 call= $6.30

Price of far month $190 call= $0.92

Cost of entering the trade and maximum risk/share= 6.3-.92=5.38

Maximum profit/share= 15-5.38= 9.62

This gives us a reward risk of $1.78, which isn't all that great, to be honest. As you can see the vagaries of option pricing affect the profit and loss calculations quite a bit. In this case, due to the existing sentiment on AAPL, perhaps the far month calls are priced lower than the near month.

I've assumed a bullish condition but this is not reflected in the prices as you can see. In reality, the far month prices, in a bullish trend, will have higher prices and it is worthwhile for you to check them out as well if you're confident of the trend in the near term.

Considerations

Given the lack of a long stock position, your margin up front is a lot less on the bull call spread. Also, since the risk is defined by the premium you pay up front, figuring out the number of contracts you wish to carry is pretty straight forward. Simply figure out how much percent of your account the max risk is and make sure it is a low enough number that won't hit your account too hard in case the trade goes south.

Of course, bullish conditions are the primary underlying factor in the trade. If the market is wildly bullish, then there's no point in executing this since you'll only be limiting your gains. However, a volatile market, which is seeing a lot of counter-trend activity, provides an excellent set of conditions for you to deploy this strategy in.

Use technical indicators to determine the short-term direction and deploy this strategy wisely.

Bear Call Spreads

Bear or short call spreads are a trade which have an inverted reward risk profile but an extremely high success rate, assuming everything is executed well. This is a strategy that a lot of professional's love, thanks to it being a steady income earner. However, risk management is absolutely critical since the potential loss you could incur is many multiples of the amount of money you stand to make.

This is a strategy where money keeps flowing in with small wins but execute something wrong and one loss will wipe everything away. A lot of beginners experience this due to getting complacent after the steady stream of money coming in.

This strategy is for sideways markets which are at a resistance zone or bearish markets. While selling a call is the best way to take advantage of a bear market, it is unlikely your broker will allow you to do this right off the bat. Hence, the bear call spread is an excellent strategy to deploy in such times.

How it Works

With a bear call spread, you will be writing an at the money or slightly out of the money call and buying a well out of the money option. Thus, on entering the trade, you will receive the premium from the lower strike price call and pay the lesser premium of the higher strike price call.

This is also the amount of your maximum profit on the trade. If the underlying stock increases in price beyond the first call, you will need to exercise your higher strike price call to buy the shares to fulfill the lower call being exercised. Thus, it is vital that your strike prices are close

21

together and not too far apart, or else your trade will be stuck in a no man's land.

All of this is better illustrated via an example. AAPL is currently trading at $173.30 and the closest at the money call is $175, priced at $4.75. Now, let's assume $175 is a major resistance and that the stock is certain to turn back downwards once it reaches here. We write a call at $175 and earn the $4.75 premium.

It is a good idea to buy calls which are two steps past the lower strike price level. At this point in time, the strike price that is two steps away is the $180 call, which can be bought for $2.84.

Cost of trade entry/maximum profit per share= Premium received from writing lower call- Premium paid to purchase higher call= 4.75- 2.84= $1.91/ share.

Maximum loss= Strike price of higher call- strike price of lower call-net premium received on trade entry= 180-175-1.91= $3.09/share.

As you can see, the reward risk is inverted with this strategy. Now, the best-case scenario for this trade is for both options to expire out of the money. In that case, you don't need to bother exercising either one of them.

The no man's land scenario is if the lower call moves into the money but the higher call doesn't. In this case, you'll have to buy the shares yourself, physically, at whatever the market price is and deliver the shares thanks to the lower call being exercised.

The worst-case scenario is price moving past the higher call, in which case you'll need to exercise it and deliver it. You'll obviously eat the entire loss in this case. This is why it is very important to make sure the price is in a strong bear trend or is near a strong resistance from which it will turn downwards.

Given the risk of this strategy, I personally recommend beginners to stick to options which are in the current month, instead of trying to capture the time decay of near month options. The additional time risk is too much and most beginners will not be able to manage risk well enough to stomach such losses.

Considerations

Your biggest concern with the bear call spread is the risk. Sure, you could widen the gap between the lower and higher call but to do so, you must be completely certain that the probability of price rising beyond the lower call is low. As always, market conditions play a huge role and you must be aware of these at all times.

What if you happen to be wrong about your market premise? What if, instead of being bearish, it turns out that the market makes a bull move? Well, this is where the adjustment comes into play.

You could flip your bear spread into a bull spread or, in the case of an expected bull market turning bearish, you could turn a bull spread into a bearish tone. As always, the call levels are important. Needless to say, you need to buy and sell the same number of contracts and both legs of the trade must belong to the same calendar month.

Don't get fancy and try to arbitrage different months or make a volatility play. If you don't know what that sentence meant then don't worry. It was aimed at those traders who know just enough to trip themselves up.

Stick to the basics of these strategies and you'll find yourself making money consistently. If you are wondering if it's possible to leverage calls with different month expiry dates successfully, then yes, it is possible. This is what the calendar spread trade is all about.

CHAPTER 3:

Advanced Strategies

The Long Straddle

This strategy applies when you buy a call and put option at the same time. The two options are always derived from the same underlying assets. They also share an expiration date and strike price. You can use this strategy when you are certain that amount charged on the security might increase, or fall beyond certain ranges that are considered normal. The long straddle ensures that you get unlimited profits from trade while keeping the losses to the minimum.

A modification of this type of strategy is when you acquire a put contract that is termed as out of the money, then also acquire a call contract that is also out of the money concurrently, with similar expiration and similar equity or base stock. Traders employ this method each time they are expecting large changes in the underlying commodity but very unsure about the direction of this movement. This is known as the long strangle strategy. Most investors use this in the place of the long straddle strategy because it limits losses more and the options always cost less since they are out of the money.

The Married Put

In this strategy, you buy an asset or security then also buy options that represent the shares you have bought. This then creates a platform for trading shares with pre-estimated strike charges. This strategy is often employed by people who wish to minimize the downside risk of owning a certain stock.

The married put works similar to an insurance policy. It specifies the lowest price that a given option can reach in case the prices reduce significantly. A good example of this is when you purchase 100 shares from a certain stock company, then open a put position on the same shares. This gives you the opportunity to raise the potential upside on each trade while cutting down the bad effects on the downside. One disadvantage of this strategy is that if the stock value does not fall, you will lose an investment that is equivalent to the premium paid for the position.

Bear Put Spread

This is also a vertical kind of strategy that allows you to buy more than one put option at the same time. The intention of using this strategy is to purchase the options at a specific strike price then exercise them at a relatively lower price. The options you use in this strategy must come from the same underlying security. They should also bear the same expiration date. The bear put strategy is the direct opposite of the bull call spread. It is often applied to markets where the value of the underlying security is expected to decrease. It also limits the gains and losses of each options contract.

The Protective Collar Strategy

This is accomplished through buying a put contract that is way out of the money, then starting a sell contract for a call option which is considered as out of the money also, concurrently. These two options are traded using the same expiration date and underlying security. Investors employ it when they have made good gains from a long stock position.

The protective collar reduces the downside risk of trading a particular option while allowing you to sell your shares at higher costs.

Long Call Butterfly Spread

Most of the strategies we have deliberated only combine two contract positions and feature two strike prices. The long call butterfly strategy is unique in the sense that it features three different strike prices. It combines the bull and bear strategies and the options used are of the same expiration dates. These are also derived from the same underlying security.

One example of this strategy is when you make a purchase of a call contract that seems in the money at a significantly small strike amount, sell double call options that are at the money and buy one call option that is out of the money. This results in a good net profit and is known as a call fly. The long call butterfly spread strategy is mostly used by investors who anticipate very little change in the stock price before the expiration.

The Iron Condor Strategy

This is also another strategy that combines the bear call and bull put strategies. It is derived through selling one put contract, which is considered out of the money than buying a single put option, which is also termed to be out of the money with strike costs that are relatively low. It also entails selling a single call contract and purchasing another call contract at strike costs that are quite high. These four spreads share similar underlying security; they have a similar exercise date with the same size of the spread.

The iron condor allows traders to earn some premium from this setup. It is commonly used in stocks that have low volatility. Traders love this strategy because it creates a high possibility of generating good premium amounts. Maximum returns are obtained as the trading gap increases. As the stock value moves away from the strike prices, the loss also increases.

This strategy can be combined with the butterfly spread to form an iron butterfly strategy where you sell a put option that is at the money, get a put contract, which is out of the money, write a call contract that has at the money characteristics then also buy one call contract that is out of the money. This strategy is different from the ordinary butterfly spread because it utilizes both put and call options. Each option performs a specific task in the contract. For instance, the call option that is out of t money shields the contract against an unlimited downside while the put option that has out of the money attributes shields the contract from short strike costs Profits realized from this kind of strategy depends on the strike prices set by the investor for each option.

CHAPTER 4:

Beginners Common Mistakes.

T rading options are more involved than trading stocks, so there are ample opportunities to make mistakes. It's important to take the approach of going small and slow at first so that you don't lose the shirt off your back. That said, if you run into mistakes don't get too down about it. Dust yourself off and get up to fight another day. With that said, let's have a look at some common mistakes and how to avoid them.

Putting all your eggs in one basket

While there is a difference between investing and trading, as traders can learn a few things from our investor brothers (and most people are a little of both anyway). Don't let everything ride on one trade. If you take all the money you have and invest it in buying options for one stock, you're making a big mistake.

Doing that is very risky, and as a beginning trader, you're going to want to mitigate your risk as much as possible. Betting on one stock may pay off sometimes, but more times than not it's going to lead you into bankruptcy territory.

Investing more than you can

It's easy to get excited about options trading. The chances to make fast money and the requirements that you analyze the markets can be very enticing. Oftentimes that leads people into getting more excited than they should. A good rule to follow with investing is to make sure that you're setting aside enough money to cover living expenses every month, with a security fund for emergencies.

Don't bet the farm on some sure thing by convincing yourself that you'll be able to make back twice as much money and so cover your expenses. Things don't always work out.

Going all in before you're ready

Another mistake is failing to take the time to learn options trading in real time. Just like getting overly excited can cause people to bet too much money or put all their money on one stock, some people are impatient and don't want to take the time to learn the options markets by selling covered calls. It's best to start with covered calls and then move slowly to small deals buying call options. Leave put options until you've gained some experience.

Failure to study the markets

Remember, you need to be truly educated to make good options trades. That means you'll need to know a lot about the companies that you're either trying to profit from or that you're shorting. Options trading isn't possible without some level of guesswork, but make your guesses educated guesses, and don't rely too much on hunches.

Not Getting Enough Time Value

Oftentimes, whether you're trading puts or calls, the time value is important. A stock may need an adequate window of time in order to beat the stock price whether it's going above it or plunging below it. When you're starting out and don't know the markets as well as a seasoned trader, you should stick to options you can buy that have a longer time period before expiring.

Not having adequate liquidity

Sometimes beginning investors overestimate their ability to play the options markets. Remember that if you buy an option, to make it work for you-you're going to need money on hand to buy stocks when the iron is hot.

And you're going to need to buy 100 shares for every option contract. Before entering into the contract, make sure that you're going to be able to exercise your option.

Not having a grip on volatility

If you don't understand volatility and its relation to premium pricing, you may end up making bad trades.

Failing to have a plan

Trading seems exciting, and when you're trading, you may lose the investors mentality. However, traders need to have a strategic plan as much as investors do. Before trading, make sure that you have everything in place, including knowing what your goals are for the trades, having pre-planned exit strategies, developing criteria for getting into a trade so that you're not doing on a whim or based on emotion.

Ignoring Expiration Dates

It sounds crazy, but many beginners don't keep track of the expiration date. Would you hate to see a stock go up in price, and then hope it keeps going up, and it does, only to find out that your expiration date passed before you exercised your option?

Overleveraging

It's easy to spend huge amounts of money in small increments. This is true when it comes to trading options. Since stocks are more expensive, it's possible to get seduced by purchasing low priced options. After all, options are available at a fraction of the cost that is required to buy stocks. And you might keep on purchasing them until you're overleveraged.

Buying cheap options

In many cases, buying cheap things isn't a good strategy. If you're buying a used car, while you might occasionally find a great car that is a good buy, in most cases a car is cheap for a reason. The same applies to options trading. When it comes to options, a cheap premium probably denotes the option is out of the money. Sure, you save some money on a cheap premium, but when the expiration date comes, you might see the real reason the option contract was a cheap buy. Of course, as we described earlier, there may be cases where cheap options have the capacity to rebound and become profitable by the time the expiry date arrives. But taking chances like that is best left to experienced traders.

Giving in to panic

Remember that you have the right to buy or sell a stock if you've purchased an option. Some beginners panic and exercise their right far too early. This can happen because of fears that they'll be missing out an opportunity with a call option, or because of fears that a stock won't keep going down on a put.

Not Knowing how much cash you can afford to lose

Going into options trading blindly is not a smart move. With each option trade you make, you need to have a clear idea of how much cash you have on hand to cover losses and exercising your options. You'll also want to know how much cash you can afford to lose if things go south.

Jumping into puts without enough experience and cash to cover losses

Remember if you're selling puts, you will have to buy the stock at the strike price if the buyer exercises their option. This is a huge risk. The stock could have plunged in value, and you're going to have to buy the stock at the strike price, possibly leaving you with huge losses. Don't go into selling puts with your eyes closed, in fact, beginners are better off avoiding selling puts. But if you must do it, make sure you can absorb the losses when you bet wrong.

Piling it on

Most beginner mistakes are related to panic. If you're looking at losses on options, some beginners double and triple up hoping to make it up when things turn better. Instead, they end up losing more money. Instead of giving in to panic, learn when to cut your losses and re-evaluate your trading strategy.

Staying in a written contract when you should get out

If you've sold an option and it's looking like you might face a loss, you can always get out of it by selling.

CHAPTER 5:

Fundamental Analysis with Options Trading

O ptional trading has grown significantly, even in the selling of stocks. The traders in this market care about the future growth of the business and not the present as opposed to the usual stock exchange. In this practice, one acquires the right to buy a stock but not the obligation. However, it should be before a certain maturation period. By the word obligation, it means that you are not mandated or forced to buy but is optional. This practice is a contract because it has the maturation period which the trader should follow.

You have to know the critical definition of some of the terms of this trading. These terms will prove significant in realizing the price trend of this trade. Remember that your main aim in the business is to have less value future contracts of buying an asset. You need to follow keenly on information regarding the assets to transact because their amount depends a lot on the premium you pay. The following are some of the terms found in this market.

There is a capped style option. This business is usually practiced when you are already aware of the asset's price. Therefore, you can quickly evaluate the profit you will gain at the end of the maturation date. The risk of trading is also significantly reduced, and you can examine the right amount to use for the business. Always remember that this business is related to forecasting of the future price and having the right to buy the assets with no obligation. However, you may wonder who facilitates such actions. It is not a broker as many of you may think but is an option writer. In simple, this person may be called the seller of an option. He or she is the mastermind of the whole process and will direct you on how to calculate the maturity value. The person also is in charge of receiving the premium. One extra thing with him is that he is obliged to buy the assets or the underlying security at the mandated price.

Sometimes due to the volatility of the market, you fear that the market will elapse significantly. There you make the right call by choosing the options trading. If you are that guy, who postpones the trading with the hope that it will maintain its worth at the expense of a volatile market, then you are wrong. Therefore, know that you are practicing the call options. This strategy is crucial if you anticipate that the market for the stocks is going to rise beyond your budget.

Another aspect is the put option which is vice versa of the call option. That involves the seller of the shares who fears that the stock market will recede. Therefore, that seller will exercise the mandate to sell stocks at a particular price at a future date. In this case, the stock value falls below the following amount. That future price is referred to as the strike price. It is thus the value that is realized at that scheduled times which the buyer or seller expects. More straightforward to say, is the value bought or sold over that specified period where you made either a call or put option. That price usually is exercised before the contract matures.

Everyone deserves the credit for their work even the option writer too. Therefore, that credit is costly in terms of payments. You have to pay that individual an optional premium. That price is realized per the agreement between you and the optional writer. That right, you are buying or selling you have to secure it with the premiums paid. Otherwise, it will be reserved for somebody else.

You have to gauge the profit you will take in the optional trading. Therefore, some terms like the intrinsic value should not escape your ears. This value is calculated by subtracting the value of the underlying stocks with the strike price. Remember that this trading is a derivative organ that depends on the amount of the fundamental asset. That fundamental has its market index, which must be less in case of call up or less in case of put up option.

Extrinsic value is another significant segment in this type of market. It is the value of that right against the intrinsic value. This trading is usually regarded as a time value fixture that has fewer profits.

Assumptions and Consideration of Optional Pricing

One assumption is that the underlying price of the stock is evenly distributed. That means the logarithm in working on its value is constant. By doing so, you can anticipate what will be the strike value or the expected value of the assets. In other terms, the volatility and the trend of the market are specific. Recognize that the volatility is the sharp increase and decrease in the price of a stock. The scheme also makes the mathematical calculation of the premium and the intrinsic value operational because of that constant function.

There are no transaction costs realized in this avenue. Moreover, there are no taxes evaluated which are calculated alongside the striking value. Otherwise, the tax and transaction costs will influence the intrinsic value reached. Therefore, by including those in the final value, there will be a sensitivity of the change in the financial instruments. Value relative to the price of the underlying assets.

There are no dividends too in this security. The bonus would operate just like the taxes and the transaction costs. That is to mean if they are included, the final value will be different from the expected. They too have to be paid per year, and it is practical to remove the dividends so that one can reach the accurate results.

The risks free rate is assumed as constant. This rate is typically associated with government subsidies or incentives. If these aspects were included, they would manipulate the results of the outcomes negatively.

Stock trading is also thought to be continuous. For you to oversee that future settlement of trade, it means that the securities will continue even at a following date. If the stocks were not continuous, then it would pose a threat to those traders with buying shares at future expectations.

CHAPTER 6:

Technical Analysis with Options Trading

Technical analysis is increasingly becoming a favored viewpoint to trading, gratitude in part to the development in trading platforms as well as charting package. Nonetheless, a new trader comprehending technical analysis as well as how it can assist in foreseeing market trends can be challenging and daunting.

Technical analysis basically involves studying the manner in which prices move within a market, in such a way that traders use patterns from historic charts and indicators to foresee the impending market trends. It is a visual reflection of the present and past performance of a given market and it enables traders to make use of this information in the fashion of indicators, patterns, as well as price action, inform and guide forthcoming trends before getting into a trade.

Here, we focus on the basics of technical analysis and consequently how it can be put into use in trading.

Comprehending Technical Analysis

The technical analysis mainly involves interpreting patterns in charts. Traders use historic data that solely depends on volume and price and consequently use the information they acquire to spot lucrative opportunities to trade based on familiar or habitual patterns in the market. Charts are exposed to a variety of indicators to establish points of entry and exit to enable traders to maximize the potential of a trade at a ratio of good risk to rewards.

In as much as the people who support fundamental analysis have a belief that economic factor mainly contributes to market movements; technical analysis traders insist that olden trends are helpful in foreseeing price movements in the future. In as much as these styles of trade vary, comprehending the disparity between technical and fundamental analysis as well as how to collaborate them can be very advantageous in the long run.

How Technical Analysis Can Help Traders

Numerous trades have approved technical analysis as an instrument for managing risks, which can be a major setback. As soon as a trader comprehends the principles and concepts of technical analysis, he/she can use it in virtually any market, thus making it an adjustable analytical instrument. As fundamental analysis seeks to identify a market's intrinsic value, the technical analysis seeks to spot trends that can suitably be caused by basic fundamentals.

Technical analysis has the following benefits:

•It can be used as an independent method.

•It is applicable to any market using any timespan.

•Technical analysis enables traders to spot patterns in the market.

Using Charts in Technical Analysis

Technical analysis is centered around charts. This is simply because the only way to gauge a market's past and current performance is by analysis the price; this is where you kick off the process of analyzing the ability of a trade. It is possible to represent price action on a chart because it is the most censorable indicator of the impacts of the price.

Charts are useful in finding the general trend, regardless of whether there is a downward or upward trend over a short or long term or to discover rage bound circumstances. The most known types of technical analysis charts include candlestick charts, line charts, and bar charts.

Whenever you use a bar or candlestick chart, every period will feed the technical analyst with information on the high and low of the period, the price where it started and also the close. Candlestick analysis is preferable the patterns as well as how they are interconnected can help in predicting the direction of the price in the future.

As soon as a trader comprehends the fundamentals of charting, they can use indicators to help in predicting the trend.

Technical Analysis Indicators

Technical traders use indicators whenever they are looking for windows of opportunity in the market. In as much as there are very many indicators, price, and volume-based indicators. These are useful in finding out the levels of resistance and support are, how they are breached or maintained as well as determining how long a trend is.

A trader has the ability to see the price as well as any other indicator by doing an analysis of numerous time frames ranging from a second to a month. This, in turn, gives the trader a different view of the price action.

The most known indicators in regard to technical analysis are:

•The corresponding strength indexes

•Moving averages

•Moving average divergence as well convergence

The last two indicators in the list above are usually used to spot market trends whereas the corresponding strength index is basically employed in finding out probable points of exit and entry. Indicators help traders in conducting an analysis of the market, finding entry points and doing validation of how trades have been set up.

Limitations of Technical Analysis

The major setback to the authenticity of technical analysis is the economic aspect of the efficient markets hypothesis (EMH). EMH asserts that market prices are a reflection of all past and current information, therefore, there is no way to exploit mispricing or patterns to get more profits. Fundamental analysts and economists who have a belief in efficient markets have no belief that any sort of information that can be acted on is contained in volume data and historical price, and in addition, that history does not repeat itself, instead, prices shift like an unplanned walk.

Technical analysis is also under criticism because it is applicable in some cases only because it contains a self- actualization prophecy. For instance, most traders will position their order to stop loss under the two-hundred-day motion average of a given company. Considering that a variety of traders have done that and it happens that the stock gets to this price, then the number of sell orders will be enormous and it will shove the stock downwards, approving the movement that traders were anticipating.

Thereafter, other traders will notice the reduction in price and also opt to put their positions up for sale, consequently improving the robustness of the trend. This selling pressure that is generally short-term can be regarded as self- fulfilling, however, it will have very minimal direction on where the price of assets will be a couple of weeks or months to come. To sum it up, if people employ similar signals, it could result in movements foreseen by the signal, but eventually, this main group of traders become incapable of steering price.

The Main Features of Technical Analysis

Technical analysis of options trading always shows how successful options trading has become and what normally leads to its success. It lists the number of successful trades on the option and what contributed to the success of these traders. Definitely, there are guides and trading techniques that a trader should always consider for them to achieve success. The analysis of options trade has always shown different features and the main feature we are going to discuss below.

First and foremost, we are going to talk about discipline. This is the key to any successful trade or even a project. As a trader, you need to be highly disciplined about what you are doing. It is however not so easy being disciplined up to a certain point in options trading but still for you to be successful, you must always exercise discipline in your field. You need to be highly committed to what you are doing for you to achieve the best that you need. You don't necessarily have to concentrate on one thing the whole day but the commitment that you show is very important.

You also need to learn from the losses that you encountered in the past. It is normal for all traders to record a loss at some point during the trading session. This does not mean that trading should stop. You learn from the loss, pick up and move on. No shortcut. You should be in a position to accept the losses and carry on with trade because of everyone's losses and if everyone was to panic and quit there would be no trading that would be proceeding until success is recorded. If you trade, lose and give up, there is no progress.

You should also be ready to learn. You are new in the market and you don't have a full idea about what you are doing. You just allow yourself to take lessons from the experts and be ready to apply the same tactics for you to carry on successfully. Watch what others do. How they carry out trade and respond to different matters is very important. You will realize you are gaining more and being well prepared to go for what you want. Technical analysis shows that if you are not well experienced in the field of options trading, you are only subjected to making mire errors than you work to succeed.

Be the decision-maker in your trading. Don't wait for others to decide for you what to do. Being your own decision maker allows you to carry out your trade successfully without putting blames on anyone. Learning for yourself is very important as much as you feel you need to take lessons from what is happening where you are. Nothing should influence you and dictate the decisions that you make. Take lessons but be independent in selecting what is best for you. This is the only way you can keep moving forward. Following what someone else is doing only leads you to a destination that was never meant for you.

A trading plan is another important feature of technical analysis of options trading. You should always have a trading plan of your own. Plan yourself well and decide what is best for you. You know exactly what you can handle and what you cannot handle and this means if you let someone plan for you, you risk straining to do something that is not within your level capacity. This only makes trading boring for you and that's why most traders quit and divert their attention to something else or blame someone for making them fail.

Watch how you react. Don't just react because you are supposed to react. The careless reaction is the number one cause of failure in any world of trading. You may face losses in your trade or some difficulties that come unplanned. How you react to them is what is more important. How do you handle losses? How do you respond to your client when something is not right? Being proactive helps you build good customer relationship with your clients and also help you to remain positive to keep moving on despite the challenges. Understand the market and making decisions based on your trading plans. Letting emotions take over you and control how you react will only interfere with how you participate in the market.

Develop a broad scope of learning. Don't just stick to one idea and think you are good to go. Everything needs a wide view so that you know how to attack everything from a different angle. When you have more ideas on what you are doing, you will find it easy switching to another plan when one fails. Being in a position to have several options helps you as a trader to be at room temperature with all types of trades. Open up your mind to convince different ideas in different fields.

CHAPTER 7:

Tips and Tricks of The Options Trading

Education is the key to success in any field, and knowledge is power. The best way to ensure success in options trading is to understand all the aspects relating to the trade. This comprehension will help you to know what you are doing and also improve your trading skills in the market. The points below cover all the essential aspects such as terminologies to personal qualities like discipline behavior that an upcoming trader should master to become a successful options trader.

Succeeding on Calls and Puts

Calls and puts are what enable options trading to take place. Options are assets that a trader can trade while using the value of underlying assets or securities. In an option contract, the buyer has the right or chance to buy (calls) or sell (puts) the underlying security. The buyer gets the right to trade the asset but does not have an obligation to do so. The key to succeeding on calls and puts is to understand the direction of stock concerning what he or she wants. Understanding that together with the following factors will enable a trader to experience success in calls and put, that is, options trading.

Understand Calls and Puts

Two bases of options trading apply in various options strategies, and a trader must understand them to succeed in options trading. They are; call options and put options. In a call options contract, the owner or trader has the right but not obligation to buy a certain amount of an underlying asset in a certain period at a pre-determined price. The exercise or strike price of a call option is the price an option buyer can buy an asset until the date of expiration. A call can also mean a call auction, which refers to the time when buyers put in place the maximum satisfactory price to buy. At the same time, sellers also put in place the minimum acceptable price to sell an asset or security in a trade.

A put option is the opposite of a call option because it sells the underlying security rather than buying it.

Understand Fundamental Analysis

Fundamental analysis looks at the external factors that might influence the price of an asset. It evaluates the inherent value of an asset and analyses the external influences and events that could affect the cost of the asset in the future. This analysis enables a person to study all factors and make a decision on the best asset to invest. He or she also learns which stocks or companies that associates with stocks to avoid. It helps a trader to know whether to buy a call contract or buy a put contract, depending on the results of the analysis.

Understand Technical Analysis

Technical analysis uses patterns in the market to predict future price movements. It uses price charts and statistics from the market to study and predict changes in price in the market. It only considers the patterns on the price chart of an asset or stock. A trader must understand the technical strategies, know which one suits his or her needs the best, and use it to make a profitable market and trading strategy. He or she must understand the technical indicators to be able to read and interpret charts and patters with ease. This way, he or she can be able to quickly think and analyze their situations and work within time limits. Time is valuable since the call and put market have expiration dates.

Understand the Numbers

Options trading always deal with numbers, and traders refer to their options trades in Greek terms. They use numerical terms like Vega, delta, theta, and gamma in the trades. A trader has to understand the numbers and how they function in options trading for him or her to interpret them correctly. An individual must know when a quantity refers to volatility or the trade's break-even.

Buying and Selling Calls and Puts

Unless an individual is a professional options trader, a trader should only be a buyer of contacts to limit the potential risk on what he or she has put up on the contract. An individual who sells options contracts takes a huge risk in trading. He or she gets profits from prices rising or falling.

Develop a Trading Style

A trader should develop a trading style that will suit his or her personality by choosing position trading, swing trading, or day trading. Position trading is one where an individual uses strategy that make the most of rare opportunities that come from volatility and time decay. Swing trading is where a trader bets on movements of price over some days, usually up to 30 days. Day training is where traders make small profits by buying and selling options many times during the day.

Interpret the News

Traders must be able to make solid personal resolutions that are in tune with their realities and not just following the hype in the news headlines. They must choose which information is the most useful, and if not, they must be able to ignore the temptations of investing through news coverage. They must be wise in their interpretation of all the information they receive before deciding on the options trading market.

Be Able to Manage Risks

There is high risk in options trading, and a trader must always consider all factors before and during a trade. He or she should examine their investment amount, pick the appropriate options contract as well as follow a suitable trading strategy to manage the risks. A trader should understand the technical and fundamental policies of options trading to maneuver the options trading markets wisely and safely.

He or she should use appropriate trade plans and strategies only after seriously thinking through them.

Be an Active Learner

One should continuously learn from their options trading experiences to improve on their profits as well as expertise to prevent a repeat of losses. The options market is always changing, and being an active learner will help a trader to keep up with the changes and be able to take the opportunities that come with those changes. He or she should be flexible enough also to learn to accept a loss and move on to a new market.

Patience and Discipline

A trader in options trading must have the discipline to achieve any form of success. He or she must consistently carry out research, keep records, and follow a productive routine to have a successful options strategy and trading results. A trader must also be patient in situations where they are waiting for an opportunity to present itself instead of chasing after every market movement. He or she must control his or her emotions when taking part in options trading to avoid making risky decisions.

Cash Allocation

A trader has to invest their money wisely when it comes to options trading. A trader should set aside a certain amount, of which only 10 to 20% should in a single contract. Options trading is a precarious business. A trader should always be careful not to lose all their money at once.

In the Money Options and Out of the Money Options

One who buys an In-the-money-option buys a contract that has an inherent value, and the buyer pays for this value at the contract price.

OPTIONS TRADING STRATEGIES

A trader who buys an Out-of-the-money-option obtains it at a lower price because the asset price is yet to reach the strike price, which will, in turn, improve the inherent value.

Be Simple

One should make their trading as simple as possible and avoid using sophisticated strategies. A person who is compounded risks losing money from the various pitfalls of different approaches when he or she uses strategies that are clearly too complex.

Time Constraints

Options deal with dates of expiration, so a trader has to know the price moves of an asset before investing to minimize the risk of losses. The price moves should have strong trends and volume that increases to stand a chance at making a profit.

Volatility in Profit

Options are investments of leverage and thus amplify the gains and losses. A trader should prepare to see vast swings of profits, as volatility is a part of options trading. A trader should also be able to interpret these swings via the use of technical indicators.

Liquid Options

Liquidity is critical in options trading as it allows possibilities of profits since buyers and sellers of an asset are always present. If an options contract is not liquid, then a trader has the risk of getting a cheap deal because no one is buying or trading it.

Mistakes to Avoid During Options Trading

There are a few mistakes that a trader should always avoid making in options trading. These mistakes can lead to damaging losses if a trader does not heed to them:

Buyback Short Strategies

Traders have to buy back short plans early to profit when a trade is in their favor. The mistake people are to assume that the deal will continue to go their way, and instead of buying back the short strategies, they sit around and wait.

Legging into Spread Trades

In this, a trader enters the various legs of multi-leg trade at the same time in hopes of making extra money from the additional leg assets.

Illiquid Options

Illiquid options mean that there is no competition for the asset since there are no buyers and sellers. It makes the asset inactive, and the resulting options will be inactive leading to considerable losses in the investment.

Chasing Markets

Similar to entering multi-leg trade, impatience and greed can lead to a person investing in numerous deals and markets while chasing after the market movements. They blindly invest because they count on the hype of an asset and end up losing a lot of money in several markets. They say the markets are like shadows, which one will never catch if they chase it. Hence, a trader should stick to a specific market with certain trading strategies and patiently wait for the market to produce an opportunity.

Exit Plan

A trader should always have an exit plan ready before even starting an options trade. The mistake many traders do is beginning to trade without an appropriate exit strategy in place. They end up incurring huge losses due to the time it takes for them to plan and implement an exit. They should consider all the factors and prepare an exit plan according to the various scenarios that can occur in the options trading market.

The points for success and potential failure in options trading provide necessary information that all traders should know. Combining the lessons from the two units above will enable a trader to achieve sustainable success in the options trading market.

CHAPTER 8:

The Psychology of An Options Trader

Options prices can move a lot over the course of short time periods. So, someone who likes to see their money protected and not losing any is not going to be suitable for options trading. Now, we all want to come out ahead, so I am not saying that you have to be happy about losing money in order to be an options trader. What you have to be willing to do is calmly observe your options losing money, and then be ready to stick it out in order to see gains return in the future. This is akin to riding a real roller coaster, but it is a financial roller coaster. Options do not slowly appreciate the way a Warren Buffett investor would hope to see. Options move big on a percentage basis, and they move fast. If you are trading multiple contracts at once, you might see yourself losing $500 and then earning $500 over a matter of a few hours. In this sense, although most options traders are not "day traders" technically speaking, you will be better off if you have a little bit of a day trading mindset.

Getting it, all started

You may be excited to jump into the market and start trading right away, but there are a few things that you will need to do first. You will need to start out with a good understanding of the basics that come with options and you need to know some of the option types that you can pick from. We talked about these topics a little bit before, but the more that you can learn about them before investing, the more success you will have. After you have had some time to understand what options are all about and what you will be getting yourself into, it is time to come up with your motivation for trading. Ask yourself how much money you are looking to make from this trade and how you would like to use that money when you have earned it. This motivation is going to help you out so much when you are in the thick of the trading and you need some help staying focus.

The trading plan is going to basically list all of the things that you want to be able to accomplish while you are trading. It can include what you expect to happen, some of your goals, the strategy that you will go with, and any other guidelines that will help you be successful. Those who decide to start investing in options without having a good plan in place will be the ones who run into a lot of risks.

You don't make emotional decisions

Since options are, by their nature, volatile, and very volatile for many stocks, coming to options trading and being really emotional about it is not a good way to approach your trading. If you are emotional, you are going to exit your trades at the wrong time in 75% of cases. You don't want to make any sudden moves when it comes to trading options. As we have said, you should have a trading plan with rules on exiting your positions, stick to those rules and you should be fine.

Be a little bit math-oriented

In order to really understand options trading and be successful, you cannot be shy about numbers. Options trading is a numbers game. That doesn't mean you have to drive over to the nearest university and get a statistics degree. But if you do understand probability and statistics, you are going to be a better options trader. Frankly, it's hard to see how you can be a good options trader without having a mind for numbers. Some math is at the core of options trading and you cannot get around it.

You are market-focused

You don't have to set up a day trading office with ten computer screens so you can be tracking everything by the moment, but if you are hoping to set up a trade and lazily come back to check it three days later, that isn't going to work with options trading. You do need to be checking your trades a few times a day. You also need to be keeping up with the latest financial and economic news, and you need to keep up with any news directly related to the companies you invest in or any news that could impact those companies. If the news does come out, you are going to need to make decisions if it's news that isn't going to be favorable to your positions. Also, you need to be checking the charts periodically so you have an idea of where things are heading for now.

Keep detailed trading journals

You don't want to get in the same situation with your options trading. It can be an emotional experience because trading options is active and fast-paced. When you have a profitable trade, it will be exciting. But you need to keep a journal to record all of your trades, in order to know exactly what the real situation is. That doesn't mean you quit if you look at your journal and find out you have a losing record, what you do is figure out why your trades aren't profitable and then make adjustments.

Take a disciplined approach

Don't just buy options for a certain stock because it feels good. You need to do research on your stocks. That will include doing fundamental analysis. This is going to mean paying attention to the history of a stock, knowing what the typical ranges are for, stock in recent history is, and also reading through the company's financial statements and prospectus.

Select a Security

This can be done by researching the finance units of major news corporations. New options traders, and particularly those who are new to trading in general, should approach options trading cautiously. Rather than diving right in, investors should get their feet wet by experimenting with a limited number of securities and options so that they can keep track of gains and losses and avoid mistakes for future investments.

Choose OTC or Regulated

Trading While this can be decided at a later stage, it is suggested here so that new investors can refer to the boards of a regulated exchange, such as the New York Stock Exchange, when choosing a put or call that is well suited to their tastes. Practiced traders can pick up an OTC option later if desired, such as a call to cover the cost of an insurance put, also known as a married put.

Select Strategies

Before beginning trading, investors will need to be sure they are familiar with a few simple strategies that can be implemented with a stock.

Examine the Market

Investors will need to study the time frame charts associated with their underlying security selection.

Purchase Options and Trade

Based upon conclusions drawn from studying time frame charts, investors will need to buy the appropriate calls or puts. At the same time, investors should choose one or two of the strategies with which they are already familiar that they believe will work well in the present market climate. If trading via a regulated exchange, options for the strategies may be selected from a list published by the exchange.

Utilizing options for trading purposes

Options can generally be utilized for trading purposes in one of two ways. First, they can be used as a type of speculation whereby those who believe they are in the know can test out their hypothesis without committing fully to their hunch.

Alternatively, those who are already flush with underlying assets can then use options trading as a type of insurance if they are unsure how some of their other investments are going to perform in either the short or the long term. Typically, options are purchased when major losses on riskier investments are expected in the near future as they allow the holder to wait and see how things proceed before getting a fair price for their investment no matter how the market falls.

Appreciate That Options Trading Is Not Simple

It is vital at this stage to recapitulate the meaning of options trading. This is a contract that grants one the right of either buying or selling a security based on the speculative value of it in a limited period of time. However, the contract is not obligatory in nature. In understanding options trading, two forms of it have to be understood; first is a call option, and the other is the put option. The two are opposites of each other. One buys the former option when one expects an asset's value to go up over time but before the deadline of expiry of the contract expires.

Read and Understand Essential Literature Available on Options Trading

Reading is part of the process of educating one's self in business. A lot of literature is currently available on various platforms for the benefit of those seeking to understand investments and avenues of investment. Success and failure stories are also hugely available, particularly on the internet where people could acquire first-hand accounts on the options trading venture.

However, reading is only helpful if the correct material is being read. Not every account of business success story is true. Some are exaggerated while others are written to arouse interest to influence people into making certain decisions for business purposes. The internet is full of hidden business activities, some of which are even hidden behind the sensational headlines of the literature resources striking people's eyes on their phones and computers. This means that knowledge is only good when it comes from the correct source.

Acquire an Understanding of the Basics of the Kinds of Trades

The trades are basically either a call option or the put option. These have to be understood well since they are the start of knowing this trade as an investment. The types of trade are the core part of the knowledge that a person can gain on options trading. All these can be explained with a desire to gain an understanding of how each of the two types of trades works. This can be achieved the desire for understanding can involve seeking mentorship or seeking consultancy firm. It can call for some level of schooling in order to begin to attain literacy, especially for those people who did not have prior knowledge of economic investments.

CHAPTER 9:

Futures Trading: The Basics

Futures are a derivative form of financial contracts that oblige the related parties to perform a transaction with an asset at a future price and date that has been predetermined. In futures trading, the buyer is required to buy, or the seller is required to sell the underlying securities at the price that has been set, no matter what is the current price in the market or what is the expiry date. The underlying assets comprise of physical commodities and other instruments of financing. The contracts of futures trading detail the exact quantity of the underlying security. They are standardized as well for facilitating trading on a futures exchange. You can use futures for speculation of trade or hedging.

What Are Futures?

Futures, also known as futures contracts, permit the traders to set the price of the underlying security or asset. All such contracts come along with dates of expiry and also set prices that are determined upfront. Futures are generally identified using the month of expiry. For instance, a gold futures contract of December will expire in the month of December. While trading futures, there are various types of contracts that you are most likely to come across.

Stock futures, for example, S&P Index

Commodity futures, for example, natural gas, crude oil, wheat, and corn

U.S. Treasury futures related to bonds and various other products

Precious metal futures for silver and gold

Currency futures including pound and euro

It is very important to identify the differences between futures and options. The contracts of options provide the holder the overall right for selling or buying the underlying security at the date of expiration. The holder of futures contracts is obliged to fulfill all the contract terms.

Pros of Futures Trading

Futures trading come along with certain pros.

The investors can use up contracts of futures for speculating right on the direction in the set price of the underlying assets.

Companies have the chance of hedging the raw material price or the products sold by them for protecting themselves from adverse movements of the price.

The contracts of futures need a deposit of only a portion of the amount of contract with the broker.

Cons of Futures Trading

Just like everything in this world, futures trading also comes along with certain cons.

Investors have the risk of losing more than the starting margin amount as futures use up leverage.

Investing in contracts of futures might lead a company that hedged to miss the favorable movements of the price.

The related margins might act as a double-edged sword. The gains will be amplified, and so will be the losses.

Using Futures

The market of futures uses up high leverage. Leverage means that a trader of futures is not required to give in 100% amount of the contract value at the time of entering into any trade. Instead of that, the broker will need an initial amount of margin, which includes a part of the total value of the contract.

The amount that will be held by a broker can differ relying on the contract size, the terms and conditions of the broker, and the investor's creditworthiness.

The exchange where the trading of futures takes place will determine whether the contract can be cash-settled or is meant for physical delivery. Any corporation can enter into a contract of physical delivery for locking in the commodity price that they need for production. But, the majority of trades of futures are from all those traders who actually speculate on the trades. The contracts are either netted or closed out- the difference between the closing price of the trade and the price of the original trade- and are settled by cash.

Speculation of Futures

A contract of futures permits a trader to speculate on the movement direction of the price of a commodity. If a trader purchases a contract of futures and the commodity price rises and starts trading much above the actual price of the contract at the date of expiry, the trader will be making a profit. Before the expiry date, the long position would be unwound with a selling trade for a similar amount at the present price, effectively closing up the long position. The difference between the contract price will be cash-settled in the brokerage account of the investor. No form of physical products will be changing hands. But the trader might also incur a loss if the price of the commodity turns out to be lower than the price of purchase that has been specified in the contract of futures.

The speculators will also be able to take a sell speculative or short position if they think that the price of the underlying security will be falling down. If the asset price actually declines, the trader will be taking an offset position for closing the futures contract. Once again, the difference will get settled at the expiry date of the futures contract. An investor can make a profit when the price of the underlying asset is below the price of the contract and will incur a loss of the present price is more than the price of the contract.

It is very important to note that margin trading will permit a larger position than the actual amount held by the account of the brokerage. As the final result, investing on margin can improve the percentage of profits but can also maximize the losses. For example, when a trader has a brokerage account balance of $5,000, and he is in a trade for a position of $50,000 in crude oil. If the oil price moves in the opposite direction of the trade, the trader will incur a loss that can even exceed the $5,000 margin amount of the account. In such a case, the broker will be making a margin call for additional funds that needs to be deposited for covering the losses of the market.

Futures Hedging

Futures can be used up for hedging the movement of the price of the underlying security. The primary goal here is to prevent losses from the potential nature of unfavorable changes in price rather than speculating. Most of the companies that opt for hedges are producing or using the underlying security. For instance, a farmer of corn can start using futures to lock in a particular selling price for their crop. By doing this, he can potentially cut down the risk and also guarantee that he can receive a fixed amount of price. If by chance, the corn price falls down, the company will be gaining on the hedges for offsetting the losses from selling the crop in the market. With such a form of loss and gain offsetting one another, hedging can effectively lock in a great price in the market.

Futures Regulation

The markets of futures are being regulated by the CFTC or Commodity Futures Trading Commission. CFTC is a form of a federal agency that was set up by Congress in the year 1974 to ensure integrity in the market price of futures. It also included the prevention of abusive practices related to trading, regulation of the brokerage firms that are related to futures trading, and prevention of fraud.

Example of Futures Trading

Suppose a trader is willing to speculate on the crude oil price by entering a position in the contract of futures in the month of May. He enters the position with the expectation that the crude oil price will go up by the end of the year. The crude oil futures of December are being traded at $50, and the trader fixes in the contract at that price. As crude oil is traded in the increment of 1,000 barrels, the trader is now holding a position that is worth $50,000 in crude oil ($50 x 1,000 = $50,000). But the trader is only required to pay out a part of the total amount upfront, the initial amount margin that is needed to be deposited with the related broker.

In the time period between May to December, the crude oil price will fluctuate exactly as the futures contract price. In case the price of crude oil turns out to be too volatile in nature, the broker might ask out for extra funds that need to be deposited into the account of margin. In the month of December, the expiry date of the futures contract is approaching, which is the third Friday of that month. The overall price of crude oil rose to $65. Now, the trader sells out the original futures cOntracts for exiting his position. The total difference will be cash-settled. They will earn a total of $15,000, excluding the commissions and fees of the broker ($65 - $50 =$15, $15 x 1,000 = $15,000).

But, if the price of crude oil came down to $40 in place of rising up to $65, the trader will be losing $10,000 ($50 - $40 =$10, $10 x 1,000 = $10,000).

Futures is a great form of investment when used in the proper way. You need to determine the market conditions properly for gaining profits.

CHAPTER 10:

Forex Trading: The Basics

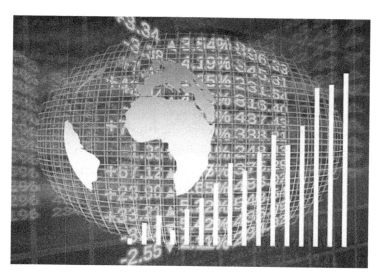

Instead of trading currencies directly to avoid high potential risks, you can also trade them via options. A Forex option is a derivative of Forex /currency trading. It is also important to know that forex options trading is simply a combination of traditional options and currency. All the terms and principles of options trading apply; the only that changes are the financial instrument.

What Is an FX Option?

An FX option acts the same way as any other options contract, except you are trading currencies. Here, you (buyer) have the right to purchase an underlying currency and hold on to it for a period at a price determined with the seller (the strike price). Again, the strike price is set when the contract is drawn. It is also important to note that the owner of the FX option has the right to exercise or not to exercise the option at maturity, while the seller is bound to sell the underlying currency to the FX trader. The amount of money paid to buy the option is also called the premium.

There are a lot of factors that come into play when trying to calculate the premium price of an FX option. But, most often, experts use a statistical or probability assumption approach to help figure it out. In FX option, a premium means two main things for both parties involved in the trade: an opportunity risk for the selling party if the other party exercises the right and buys the underlying security.

At the other end, it represents the opportunity to own the underlying currency at the contract's predetermined strike price. Upon maturity, where it was profitable, the holder of the FX option enjoys the privilege of garnering from the trade an intrinsic value for the currency. This value depends on the correlation between the currency's price and the option's strike price, and the time value can be measured by the difference between the premium and the said intrinsic value.

Why FX Options?

There is time value for any options purchased by the buyer at a premium price. The risks associated with forex trading stem from volatility, expiration time, the price of the underlying currency, and the interest rate differentials. The premium paid for the option is sometimes very high. The option contracts cannot be resold or re-traded.

The benefits of FX options cannot be underestimated. They help reduce the potential risk of buying a currency pair; traders can trade in currencies through the options contract without necessary gaining ownership of hundreds of the currency pairs.

FX Options are also used to hedge trading positions in the forex trading market. This prevents losing the value of the underlying currency when the value goes up. Unlike the cash or futures market, it does not involve the immediate settlement of transactions.

An FX option is also used as a form of hedge to prevent losing the value of a currency pair when the market is generally falling in value.

Types of Options

Basically, there are two types of FX options trading available in the market. To do well in the current market, it is essential to understand and know how these forex options trading works.

Traditional FX Options

This is known as the vanilla FX options type, involving both call and put options. As usual, this right goes without any obligation.

For example, A EUR/USD option would provide the buyer with the right to sell €1500 and buy $ 1000 on January 2. The strike price for the option is EUR/USD 1.50. The holder of the currency pair will incur revenue in this trade if its exchange rate is not more than 1. 50.

The underlying contract will expire in the money and generate profit. Let's say that the EUR/USD has fallen to 1.00. The profit derived from the FX option will be as follows: (1.50 − 1.00) x 1,000 = 500. In this case, the holder is benefitting from the fall in currency rate.

The buyer of the option will have to tell how many options contracts they want to buy, pay the premium for the contract, and hold onto the contract until it gets in the money before exercising the due rights to buy or sell the underlying currency. The only loss here is the premium paid for the option when the option expires without any of these options exercised.

Sing Payment Options Trading (SPOT)

Single payment options (SPOT) operate just like a binary option, offering the buyer an all or nothing type of offer for placing and making associated deals. Traders receive payouts based on the probability of a prediction about current prices in the future being right or wrong.

When you expect the market to rise up, you place a call option. When your prediction comes through, then you will win the agreed profit set forth for the option.

Losses are made when the prediction for the FS options are wrong. Premium payments for SPOT are often higher than the traditional options trading for currencies. It's highly advisable that traders understand the risks and rewards associated with this type of options trading before engaging in it.

Where to Trade Forex Options

If you are looking to trade in forex options, you have to research many retail forex brokerage firms to check whether they provide that service. Due to the recent losses that many traders have been having when trading forex options, many brokers have decided to ensure that only traders with capital protection are allowed in order to cap the risks of enormous losses, especially with SPOT.

There are some brokerage firms that provide access to the option and future exchanges, while others simply provide you with an OTC contract. Prior to signing on any broker platform, ensure you examine the fees and deposit requirements for trading. Check out the CBOE to learn more about the market before placing a trade on the platform.

CHAPTER 11:

Swing Trading: The Basics

S wing trading is a simple trading philosophy, where the idea is to trade "swings" in market prices. In a commonsense kind of way, there is nothing special about swing trading because it's a buy-low and sell-high method of trading with stocks. You can also profit from a stock when the price is declining by "shorting" the stock.

So, what distinguishes swing trading from other types of trading and investing? The main distinction that is important is that swing trading is different from day trading. A day trader will enter their stock position and exit the position on the same trading day. Day traders never hold a position overnight.

Swing traders hold a position at least for a day, which means they will hold their position at a minimum overnight. Then they will wait for an anticipated "swing" in the stock price to exit the position. This time frame can be days to weeks, or out to a few months' maximum.

A swing trader also differs from an investor, since at the most, the swing trader is going to be getting out of a position in a few months. Investors are in it for the long haul and often put their money in companies that they strongly believe in. Alternatively, they are looking to build a "nest egg" over a time period of one to three decades or even more.

Swing traders don't particularly care about the companies they buy stock in. They are simply looking to make a short-term profit. So, although swing traders may not be hoping to make an instant profit like a day trader, they are not going to be hoping for profits from the long-term prospects of a company. A swing trader is only interested in changing stock prices. Even the reasons behind the changes in the stock prices may not be important. So, whether it's Apple or some unknown company, if it is in a big swing in stock prices, the swing trader will be interested.

The chart below shows the concept of swing trading. If you are betting on falling prices, you can earn profit following the red line in the chart. If you are betting on increasing prices, you would follow the upward trending blue line. A bet on falling prices is often referred to as being short, while a bet on rising prices means you are long on the stock. This, of course, is another difference between swing trading and investing; investors don't short stock.

Swing trading can be used in any financial market. In the chart above, we are actually showing a chart from the Forex (currency exchange) market. The principles are the same, so the specific market we are talking about doesn't really matter, which is why it works with options.

Support and Resistance

An important concept often used by swing traders is spotting support and resistance. Support refers to a local low price of the stock. It's basically a pricing floor that, for the time being, the stock price is not dropping below. To find support, you just draw straight lines on the stock chart.

The share price should touch the support level at least twice in order for it to be a valid level of support.

Resistance is a local high price. So, this is a high price level that the stock is not able to break above. Again, expect it to touch the resistance level at least twice, and drop back down, before you consider a given share price for the resistance level.

As the share price moves in between support and resistance, there are opportunities to buy-low at the support level price and then sell-high at the resistance level. And you can do the reverse in the case of shorting stock. You can enter your position at the relatively high resistance level, then exit your position at the support level.

Of course, support and resistance are not going to be valid price levels for all time, and a stock will often "break out" of support or resistance. This happens when the share price starts a declining trend and goes below the support level, or if it breaks out above the resistance level in an uptrend. These can be more opportunities to make a profit. But, when a stock price is stuck between support and resistance levels, we say it is ranging.

Trade with the Trend

The best thing to happen to a swing trader (or a trader of straight call and put options) is for a stock to enter into a unidirectional trend. So, it could be a trend in upward prices, giving you a chance to make large profits before it starts reversing. Alternatively, of course, trends can head downwards, opening up opportunities for those who are shorting the stock.

Trends can exist in many different time frames. It might only last part of a day, or it could last weeks and even months. Learning to spot trends and take advantage of them, with a sense as to when the trends are going to come to an end, is something that comes with experience and education. A new options trader can benefit by studying educational materials related to both swing and day trading so they know what to look for in stock charts to spot not only trends worth getting into, but also how to spot a trend reversal which would eat up your profits.

The chart below of AutoZone stock is a simple example of this concept. It's a dream trade, with prices going steadily up with time. But remember nothing lasts forever.

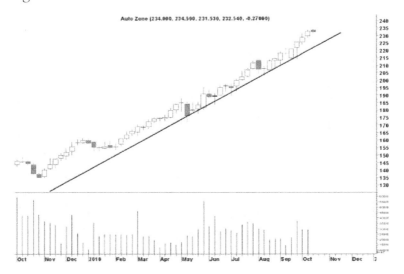

Trading with a trend is definitely something you'll want to look for as an options trader. The time scale of the trend is going to be something important, of course, because you are going to be concerned about time decay when trading options. Time decay is a concept that a swing trader does not have to worry about.

So rather than being beholden to specific rules, like saying you are going to trade options like a day trader or like a swing trader, an options trader has to be flexible. You will need to be ready to take advantage of very short term moves in stock price that only last for a day or less, and you'll also want to be in trades that can last days to weeks or even months.

Swing Trading Options

Since options are time-limited, they are a natural fit for the concept of swing trading. Although many of the advanced strategies attempt to take out the direction of share price movement from the equation, if you are buying single call or put options in order to make a profit, then you're definitely behaving at least in a qualitative sense like a swing trader.

Since put options gain in value when stock prices are declining, buying put options is like shorting stock. It's actually quite a bit more accessible, however. In order to short stock, you must have a margin account so that you can borrow shares from the broker. The basic idea of shorting stock is to borrow shares from the broker when the stock price is at a relatively high point and sell them. After this, the trader will wait for the share price to drop. Then when the share price is low enough to make a profit, the trader will buy the shares back and return them to the broker.

Of course, shorting stock using options is far easier. The reason is you never have to buy the stock to make a profit from the declining price. You simply profit from prices of put options which will increase as the stock price goes down.

Going Long on a Stock

If you believe that the price of a stock is going to rise, then you want to buy call options. So, call options represent the most straightforward or common-sense way to trade options. When you buy a call option, you are betting on that stock. Another way to say this is that you are bullish on the stock.

A good way to go about trading options is to pick a few companies and limit yourself to trading them. The reason is that you are going to have to be paying attention to the markets, company news, and general financial news for any option that you invest in. If you spread yourself too thin, you are not going to be able to stay on top of things and will find yourself getting caught up in losing trades. The best approach is to keep your trading limited in scope so that you can know what is going on. That doesn't mean you only trade a single call option; you might trade a large number of them on the same stock.

There are two ways to go about swing trading options. The first way is to look for ranging stocks that are trapped in between support and resistance. Then you can trade call and put options that move with the swings. So, the idea of this type of trading is very simple. First, you need to study a stock of interest and determine what the price levels of support and resistance are. Then, when the price drops to the support level, you buy call options. Now hold them until the price goes back up near resistance. It can be a good idea to exit your trades before the price gets all the way to resistance so that you don't end up losing some of your potential profits if the price reverses before you get rid of the options.

Trend trading call options can also be very lucrative. In this case, you are looking for significant news and developments related to the stock or even the economy at large. For example, when a company announces that it had big profits, this can be an opportunity to earn money with call options, as the price will go up by large amounts as people start snapping up the stock. When trading in this fashion, you're going to need to know how to spot trend reversals. The idea is basically the same when you identify a trend in the making, you buy call options, and then ride the trend until you are satisfied with the level of profit and sell the options.

Again, it can't be emphasized too much. You always need to take time to decay into account when trading options. So, remember that with each passing day, your options are going to lose value automatically. Check theta to find out how much value they are going to lose. And as we deliberated before, often, other factors overwhelm time decay in the short term.

CHAPTER 12:

Stock Market Investing: The Basics

Investors around the world are usually willing to transform the hard-earned money of theirs into an amount which may secure the life of theirs in the years to are available in the least possible time. Not many investment alternatives are able to provide the result which an investor seeks.

Stock Market is among the choices where it's attainable. The king of all of the investment choices wherein it's feasible to generate a lot immediately is Stock Market. Many Investor thinks that stock market investing offers them together with the scope of the optimum return in the shortest period.

Job of Stock Market for Investors

For investors, the stock market and the day trading of its are definitely the places from wherever they look ahead to get transactions, i.e. sell or buy, in the stocks they really feel confident with.

The procedure for purchasing or marketing of a stock may be accomplished in real time day trading, etc., online stock market. By comprehending the job of the stock market of stocks along with a stock trader, it's simple to recognize the fundamental working which is interested in the stock market. Nevertheless, an investor that looks ahead for removing optimum tries to collect increasingly more understanding on the topic of the stock market'.

In order to collect much better information, it's crucial for mastering the conditions active in the realm of morning trading', stockbroker', stock trader', etc. which has stock quotes & market capitalization.

Stock Quotes

Stock quotes are managed by many factors which normally include affordable wellbeing, trends in trading and spending and financial or technical report of the organization put forward to the investors by an experienced stockbroker or the company.

Industry Capitalization

Market capitalization is yet another term that can ring in the ears of yours while you're engaged in a chat whose subject is connected to the stock market. The word indicates the general values of companies or maybe stocks that are available in the stock market. With a system is able to do the calculation of market capitalization of stocks: Number of surplus shares on the market X stock quotes.

Selling and buying of Stocks

The following phase after knowing the fundamental terminologies is studying the procedures for purchasing just selling of stocks in the online stock or day trading market. Buying stocks will be the process that involves a suitable purchase quantity from a stock trader. This particular expenditure quantity is employed in spending for the entire quantity of the stocks brought together with the percentage or maybe the tax costs associated with the transaction. Investor opts for opening an investment account with stockbroker with solid close by investor's location for convenience. Nevertheless, the internet stock market has provided an alternative for an internet account to buy some stock trader that enables them to purchase without having the participation of any stockbroker.

The procedure that uses the opening of the purchase account is funding it for doing the purchases. The minute the account of yours gets the apt fund for the investment, stock buying may be done. The procedure for offering demands the stock trader to understand the stockbroker of theirs regarding the volume of shares you need selling and at what stock costs. The Internet stock market demands the trader to go into the order for sale through the investment account of theirs. When you realize the working and the proceedings of stock market investing, the success of yours in the area is unstoppable.

STOCK MARKET TIMING ADVICE AND STRATEGY

In the situation of stock market purchase, timing is essential. The main choice which is present for any profitable stock market investor is usually to focus on for the best timing for many benefits as well as a reduced amount of losses. Firms issue stocks of theirs to get money and make an investment in the company. Stocks are offered to individuals in order they can purchase and sell them. The importance of stock depends on the availability as well as demand involved, extremely like the price of another item.

Engaging in the company of stock market selling and buying regularly yields more huge gains to traders versus entering into a normal stock enterprise. You are going to discover an incredible array of stocks to pick from when any trader embarks upon trading the stocks. Amongst plenty of registered stocks, you are able to get a moving stock out there. Individuals who unwisely continuing into the marketplace are certain to think of undesirable overall performance. Enormous losses may be incurred if the stock market direction is not correctly predicted. Nevertheless, small profits are irritating to the main reason for trading in the marketplace and becoming more cash. New stock traders might end up waiting around for any considerable instant that might not actually come.

The following are very few stock market timing advices in addition to strategy,

To time The Market

Traders use industry timing to foresee at what time the markets might change the path of its. Through the usage of industry timing, traders search for to keep far from the dangerous effects of poor stock trading. While through the use of market timing, it could be instantly assumed as well as the crucial spot is generally predicted prior to time. By learning-related financial details as well as the value, the pattern of the stock market place is predicted to provide confidence for much more lucrative stock trading.

Obtaining the Perfect Timing

The goal of the individuals who want to become successful at stock investment is usually to get the best market timing. The steadiness of this direction prediction is concentrated on a variety of elements. As market timing looks like a certain method in making large profits, it is not with no critical effort. Sincere effort is recommended relating persistence in learning various industry elements in addition to constant attempt to remain educated regarding existing stock market trends. Easy speculation has to stay away from. Speculating is truly a risky move utilized whenever a sector trader hasn't made the proper research. Often traders purchase stocks based on a warm suggestion they got from somebody else. Unluckily, the vast majority of those warm recommendations eventually end up being fake since they're likely to end up provided by parties because of their own vested interests. In order to develop effective industry timing, traders need to obtain actively involved in an appraisal about the company's history consequently they could calculate the pattern via charting the motion of cost of a stock. The cost of a stock must be analyzed to produce a relatively appropriate prediction about the stock market trend. Through the use of this particular exercise, traders develop standards for at what time to purchase and at what time to promote consequently they can exactly time the stock investments of theirs.

STOCK MARKET TIPS

Appear before you leap is probably the most pertinent of all the stock market ideas provided by investment professional, do not depend on the stock market tips provided by the friend of yours, the waiter in the restaurant or maybe the brother of yours in law, but simply believe in the senses of yours when making an asset. The pre-investment research of yours must consist of careful evaluation of the market trends, the price and industry performance fluctuations of any stock to ensure you are able to select the winners. Here are a few stock market suggestions that will enable you to understand several crucial ideas of equity investments. Tip #1: Whenever you purchase a stock you're buying partial ownership in a business; also referred to as shares; these stocks provide you with a right to a component of the company's assets and profits; however, you're exempt from virtually any debts that the group might incur through the course of company.

Tip #2: You will find various kinds of stocks and they provide an assortment of characteristics. While picking out the kind of shares, you need to make sure that the stock meets the investment objectives of yours. For example, in case you're searching for a regular income, you need to pick stocks that provide regular dividends. On the flip side, in case you're searching for capital gains, you need to pick stocks that have a possibility for the substantial cost increase in the future.

Tip #3: The stock market isn't really distinct from an auction house in which the number of customers enthusiastic about a specific item typically determines the scope of cost rise

Tip #4: Stock prices are susceptible to fluctuations and based on the stock type you purchase; you might witness rather a good deal of volatility on an everyday basis

Tip #5: Companies just trade in their very own stocks once; whenever they provide the share to the public as a beginner through an IPO or perhaps initial public offering. Subsequently, the supply as well as demand factors for a specific stock as well as the company's efficiency sets the cost of the shares with no interference from the business.

Tip #6: Stocks are traded by the NYSE and stock exchanges or maybe the brand New York Stock exchange will be the main stock exchange in the nation which contains the greatest amount of blue-chip companies mentioned on it.

Tip #7: You will find 2 methods to buy a stock, you are able to wither get in contact with a stockbroking tight and start an account with them or maybe you might enlist with an internet stockbroking firm as well as to conduct stock trading as well as transactions on the internet

Tip #8: You are going to need files like the social security of yours, proof of identity and residence to start an account and have a stockbroking firm

Tip #9: The equities marketplace functions on a fundamental idea; that's a greater risk equates to a much better opportunity for reward; however, this specific process doesn't constantly hold true.

Tip #10: You are able to get info on stocks with the stock charts & tables in your daily newspaper

CHAPTER 13:

The Concept of Moneyness

The term moneyness is used in Options trading to describe the financial status of an Option. An option is said to be in the money— or profitable to exercise if its strike price is lower than the price of the underlying asset.

However, the concept of moneyness has a few different aspects to it.

Remember that the strike price is the locked-in price that the underlying stock can be bought or sold for, if exercised. Therefore, the strike price is an important factor in determining the Options value as we can compare the Options strike price with the actual market price of the stock. This relationship between the strike and actual market price determines the intrinsic value of the Option and will be a determining factor:

At the money: This is when the strike price and the stock price is the same and so it applies to both calls and puts

Near the money: As it is unlikely for the strike and actual price to exactly match any close to equality is termed near the money

In the money: This is when the strike price in a call option is below the price of the actual stock. On the other hand, with a put option, the strike price is in the money when it is above the stock price

Out of the money: This is when a call option strike price is above the stock price. With a put option, the strike price will be out of the money when it is below the stock price

As you start to practice and gain experience working with quote tables and orders, you will become very familiar with these terms. This is because you will soon become accustomed to using the relationship between the stock price and the strike price to determine if there is any intrinsic value in the Option. A thing to remember is that only options that are "in the money" will have any intrinsic value.

Indeed, an option will be said to be in the money only if it is profitable to exercise. It is out of the money if it is not profitable. This means that just because the strike price is above or below the actual price doesn't automatically make it in the money as we must always consider the cost of the premium. Also, the relationship of the underlying price to the strike price depends on the type of option involved.

Conversely for the writer of the option, the trader that is obliged to fulfill the holder's rights whether that is to buy or to sell, then they will have the opposite point of view. For the writer of the Option has taken a short position and will be out of the money when the price of the underlying asset is greater than the strike price and, in the money, when the price of the underlying asset is less than the exercise.

Similarly, the positions are reversed when we consider relative perspectives of the holder and writer of the put option. For example, if the holder of a put option has a strike price of $35 and if the underlying stock is trading at more than $35, then they would be out of the money as it would not be profitable to exercise so that the long-put position would be out of the money. However, the holders long put would be in the money if the underlying were to trade at less than $35.

But conversely, if we consider the short-put position, we will find that an underlying price of more than $35 would mean the option would not be exercised by the holder, so the writer could keep the premium and be in the money. But, if the underlying stock price were to fall below $35, then the option would be in the money from the holder's perspective as it could be exercised at a profit and the writer's short position would now be out of the money.

The following table offers a neat summary of it all.

Position	In the Money	Out of the Money
Long call	Stock > Strike	Stock < Strike
Short call	Stock < Strike	Stock > Strike
Long put	Stock < Strike	Stock > Strike
Short put	Stock > Strike	Stock < Strike

Stock = current market price of the underlying stock (variable)

Strike = the locked-in strike price of the Option (fixed)

As we can see the holder and the writer of the Options always have an opposite position except when the strike price and the underlying price are the same, then the option is at the money or near the money. This is regardless of the type of option whether it is a put or a call, or whether you are going long or short.

Open Interest

An interesting metric that is often included in quote tables for Option contracts is an indicator depicting Open interest, which is the total number of outstanding options contracts. Open interest is tallied at the end of each day.

Open interest is used as a metric for the measurement of market sentiment. It should not be misinterpreted as the number of options traded because it is not the same thing as volume as many options are traded to close out existing positions.

However, if you are speculating in short term trading of options then Open Interest is an important metric as you will want as much market interest as you can get on your option. This will make it easier to trade when you choose to exit the position as there will likely be many potential buyers.

Expiration and Exercise

Options expire at regular intervals determined by the expiration date, which is the date the option expires. Most options expire on the third Friday of a given month. However, some high-volume weekly options have expiration dates every Friday. The last time to trade the option is at the close of the market immediately before the option expires. Some European options close earlier (sometimes on a Thursday but the closing time would be specified for the option, and most broker apps track the options expiry dates and send a notification so you'd know):

The option period is the term used to denote the valid time until expiration and it starts the moment the option is made (written) and ends on the expiry day. However, there are ways to stay in the position if you want to beyond the expiry date. If you want to maintain the position you can roll by closing your current — soon to expire - open position and simultaneously make a new position at a different strike price or expiration.

Exercising your Rights

To exercise is the term used to cash in an option but the vast majority of options are never exercised. But should you want to and you have a call option giving you the right to buy shares of ABC at $100 per share, and the stock is trading at $105, all you have to do is notify your broker that you want to exercise the Option.

When exercising your option to buy the stock you will need to have the funds in your account. Almost all brokers will require that you buy — pay for the stock — before you sell.

This means that you will need sufficient funds in your account before you can exercise your position. Some brokers allow you to turn around and sell the stock immediately and you may get away with selling the stock before you pay the broker, but that type of free-riding - is frowned up.

Delivery and Settlement

When a call option on a stock is exercised, the writer has to transfer the shares to the option buyer's account at the strike price. If the writer is not covered by already owning the stock they must go and buy the shares in the open market.

However, if there is an option for cash settlement, then the person whose option is profitable receives a cash transfer payment. This is more commonly used in trading in index options.

Extrinsic and Intrinsic Value

Options have two primary sources of value. An option has intrinsic value only if it is in the money. If it is not in the money then there is no profit so no value.

Time value, on the other hand, is known as extrinsic value. This value is the difference between the option's price and the amount of intrinsic value - the amount it is in the money. The logic behind this is that the amount that an option is in the money is its intrinsic value, the profit should you claim it today.

But the option can be worth more today than the profit you would realize if you exercised it. This is an important consideration when you are hedging as you do not want to exercise the option – take the profit. Instead, you value the time remaining on the insurance value of the option. This additional time value cannot be ignored as it explains why people will often hold onto options when they are profitable to exercise. Of course, they may just be riding a trend and hoping to end up with a larger profit.

Nonetheless, it is important to realize that Options do have both extrinsic value and intrinsic value. The more you understand the components of an option's price, the better you can value the option relative to your needs.

One additional concept of Option value that we must know about is parity. When we refer to Parity with regards to an Options value, we mean the point where an option is in the money but has no time value. Options generally don't reach parity until just before expiration.

CHAPTER 14:

Treating Option Trading as A Business

Have you ever thought about all the occupations in the world? Have you considered the time and investment people put in? The owners trusted you to perform such a job.

If you are one of the owners, will you allow anyone to perform their duty without any knowledge or training? Of course, you will not think about that.

Even if you decide to do a menial job that does not require any higher education, you will still need some sort of training. As menial as a dishwashing job may be, it has its techniques, the same way it is when you want to perform a surgery. Both jobs are very different, but they do require you to follow instruction.

In the same manner, a person who finds a website and starts trading options in the market without any prior knowledge and instruction may succeed but for a while. However, "this career" will be short-lived, as his funds will disappear suddenly.

On second thought, won't it be better to take your time and learn everything required to be a good trader? The result is always impressive, but the process requires dedication.

Well, trading is very different from other occupations or business, although it is still a business. Running your Options Trading as a business will go a long way rather than just desiring to make huge money and improve your lifestyle.

Most traders start on the wrong foot, and I want to avail you this opportunity to start on the right path.

You must recognize that Options Trading is not like taking a trip to one of the prominent casinos in Las Vegas. Treating Options Trading as a business requires planning and structure.

It also involves a cost to get the business running successfully. To begin as a successful options trader, you must run and view Options Trading as a full-term business.

Cost of Running Options Trading as a business

Similar to any kind of business, the easiest means of making a profit is by generating more profits than your costs. Undoubtedly, you will agree to this statement because if you continue to lose money, you will ultimately reap off your business.

All professional traders will tell you never to allow your cost or capital to become larger than your revenue or profit.

For options trading, the primary cost of running it as a business is losing trades. Does that sound right? Well, it should if you want to be a successful trader. At the back of your mind, always consider losing trade as your cost of trading options.

It is important to see them that way and never allow your emotions to becloud or influence your judgment. At times, you must think like a restaurant owner, who does not get unhappy or angry because customers made a re-order of their food.

Any trader who told you he or she hasn't lost trade in their entire career is simply lying to your face. Every successful trader on Earth, irrespective of how profitable they may be, might have lost a trade once in their career.

So, when you begin your journey, you shouldn't be perturbed by the temporary losses. They are unavoidable, but you can always beat the market. Furthermore, you must be prepared to deal with them at all cost

Steps to Starting Trading Options as a Business

Interestingly, stock options trading offers great opportunity to reap profits because you can control about 100 shares for each stock option with your risk limited to the option price. There are no much trading instruments, which can offer such leverage with limited risk.

However, upcoming option traders find it hard to make a profit, because they lack the skill to trade options like any business. Well, if you follow the steps below, then you are sure on the right path to trading options like any professional. So how do you begin your options trading as a business?

First, you need to find a professional options broker in the market. Today, we have numerous brokers (both real and fake) looking for beginners like you to make an investment.

However, you have to be diligent in searching the internet and conducting interviews where applicable. If you know anyone who has been in the market, you can ask for a recommendation.

If you decide to take the first route, then you must ask the broker how long they have been trading options. Ask them their take on the difference between Ratio Back spread and Calendar Spread.

The truth remains that working with an experienced broker is a valuable asset, especially in a volatile market like the Options market.

Secondly, choose a reliable trading platform, which incorporates your brokerage account, price charts, and offer the buy/sell features openly with your broker. Successful businesses take time and adequate planning to succeed; this you must be willing to do if you want to thrive in options trading.

Ensure you perform a background check on the various trading platform, read appraisals of their earlier clients to ascertain if they are the right choice. You will not want your business to hit the ground before you begin.

Thirdly, once you are convinced of the platform, you can then open your Options trading account. Different brokerages have their minimum amount you can use to open an account.

Some offer as little as $1000; however, averagely, most brokerage accepts $5000 in order to open an account. Nevertheless, these always come with certain limitation to your account.

Fourthly, you should set up two different screens – one to track your underlying stock after setting up the price charts and the second for the stock symbols. Additionally, you need another separate screen to view the option quotes of the stock you are tracking.

Do you have an Options Trading Business Plan?

Perhaps you have heard that. However, what is the requirement for anyone to succeed in this market?

Top traders, along with investors, will always place discipline as the key to success.

That is the truth because without discipline, you will allow a losing trade develop into a portfolio murderer.

Two essential ingredients if you want to succeed in options trading are education and knowledge.

However, your efforts and money will be in total vain if you lack the discipline in following a prearranged trading plan.

For some, trading options come with frustrating challenges, while others get a lifetime financial reward. Where you fall among these two groups, depends on you.

Writing a solid trading plan is essential, as it will expose your trading approach, risk, and money management tactics.

A sound training plan will highlight the kind of trades to take, those to avoid, your risk control, and trade management.

After gathering all knowledge, you need to spend a large chunk of your time on your trading plan. Do you want to treat Options Trading as a business?

You cannot run away from having a practical business plan for your business. It is the bedrock of you building a successful option-trading career.

Fact: Most upcoming option traders start to fail when they neglect to have a comprehensive trading plan. For others who start but fail to complete all the necessary plans, at the end regret it.

Timing your trade and control your risk is too important to be neglected in your trading plan if you want to trade profitably and operate Options Trading as a business.

Business Sample Plan for Options Trading

This business plan will integrate different aspects of trading you may be familiar with if you are a professional. However, if you are a beginner and new to the trading environment, then it will be more beneficial.

As already stated, trading options is similar to any kind of business. It is not enough to think that trading is a business, but you must put into consideration every detail that has the capacity of influencing your success and affecting your overall cost-effectiveness. There are specific costs that need to be covered if you want to take it as a full-term business.

Perhaps, you will need computer costs, tax implications, price data fees, and fees for using the trading platform. Your electricity bills aren't exempted from it because it has an impact on your profit.

Options trading plan is a documentation of everything you require to operate your trading business smoothly. It includes your money management, trading strategy, what to trade, and the valuation process of trades. Before you consider creating your trading plan, you need to define your objectives or goals.

What are your goals?

What do you want to achieve in this newfound business? What are your personal developments, financial, or trading goals?

Financial goals

As a yardstick, what profit are you expecting per month or year?

Are you going to use different strategies when faced with different market situations?

Personal development goals

How will you improve yourself?

What will you do if your financial goals aren't met?

What will be your reaction to drawdown periods?

Using Your Options Trading Plan

When you have a comprehensive trading plan, it shows strategies and restrictions for your trading activities. Practical use of your trading plan is to enable you to manage your risk exposure and money. Because of this, it is important to include information on the capital to use and the level of risk that won't affect you.

Once you follow your plan and use your money judiciously, you will not be a victim of the biggest mistakes traders and investors make. With this, you won't use scared money as the case of most investors.

If you decide to trade with money you can't afford to lose or meant for another purpose, you will make rational decisions while trading. Although it is hard to take emotion during Options Trading, it will pay you better to remain focus on the primary motive of your trading.

Once emotion sets in, you start losing your focus and begin to make illogical decisions. For instance, this could lead to you chasing losses from earlier trades, which has gone wrong.

However, if you have a plan, follow it, and stick to use your investment capital, you stand a better possibility of keeping your emotions in check.

Likewise, you must stick to the risk level outlined in your trading plan. If you decide that low-risk trades are your best strategy, there isn't any need for exposing yourself to trades with higher risks.

At times, it is tempting to trade with higher risks after making some loss with the "believe" of fixing them. Most times, this does not turn out as expected. However, you don't have to cage yourself; you should consider stepping out of your comfort, especially when the risk involved isn't high.

CHAPTER 15:

Hedging and Speculation

T wo of the biggest reasons why an investor might be interested in trading options in the first place is because of the factors of speculation and hedging. This part will focus on how exactly speculation and hedging work within the broader scope of options trading. You may find yourself in a position where you are already using these tactics in your trading life, but you should still read this sector so that you can find new ways to use these techniques in a way to expand your current trading strategies. If you are already using these strategies in your current options trading strategies, it's probably best to think of this part as one that can deepen your understanding of these concepts and hone concepts with which you may already be familiar.

What is Speculation?

The first concept that we're going to discuss is speculation. Speculation in the broadest sense is the process that an investor takes on a stock with the expectation that there is a high potential to lose large amounts of money extremely quickly. The concept of speculation is largely the reason why options trading has the reputation of being one of the riskiest ways that you can invest your money. While this concept of trading is certainly risky in nature, it's important to understand that the money that is anticipated to be lost is typically seen as being won again in even larger amounts once the options have reached their maturation. It's important to understand that it can sometimes be difficult to decipher whether or not the intention behind the motivation to conduct a trade can be considered speculative or not. Some factors that can distinguish a speculation from a typical investment include the amount of leverage that is involved in the transaction, how long the investor plans to hold the stock, and the nature of the asset as a whole.

Options in general are considered be pretty speculative in nature because prior to purchasing an option you have to choose which direction you're going to purchase the asset as well as how much the price is going to increase or decrease over a certain period of time. Of course, due to the risky nature of options trading in general you might be asking yourself why people even engage in the act of speculation to begin with, it being regarded as such as a risky endeavor. The biggest reason why investors are most interested in options and speculation is that the risks are usually outweighed by the rewards. Especially if you can speculate well, then it's likely that you are going to be great at options trading. One of the biggest reasons why options are speculative is because of the high levels of leveraging that often accompanies speculation. With options, you are able to purchase stake in something that is much cheaper than purchasing a regular stock at its full market price. This leveraging against the price of the entire stock is what largely allows an investor to own a position in the stock, rather than the entire stock itself. Let's take a look at an example. Let's say that there is an investor who is looking at a particular stock that costs fifty-dollars per share. This is a hefty sum of money, especially because this particular investor only has two-thousand dollars to spend on investments at this particular moment in time. You have two options here. You can either decide to purchase forty shares of this particular stock at the fifty-dollar going rate, or you can instead purchase options of the stock. If you decide to engage in the latter, this means that you will be purchasing one-thousand options shares of the stock instead of only forty. Of course, options are going to amplify both the losses and the gains that you're going to see

What is Hedging?

When you hedge an option, what you're essentially doing is providing yourself with security in other investments that are already in your portfolio. If we look at an example, this concept will become more accessible to you. For example, let's say that you own some stocks. They're high priced, and you really have no idea of knowing whether or not they're going to appreciate over the long-term; however, you know that you want to stick with this stock for the long-term because this is part of your long-term investment strategy. Instead of simply hoping for the best even though you know that company in which you've invested is going through a rough patch, you are looking for more security. You decide that you're going to invest in an option, but in a way that counteracts the decisions that you've made regarding the activity that you've already invested in with the long-term stocks that you already own. Let's take a look at this concept on a more in-depth level, because whether you are aware of it or not, hedging is considered to be an advanced options trading strategy, even though the concepts within it are fairly straightforward.

How to Hedge an Option

Some common examples of hedging include taking out insurance that will minimize your income's exposure to risk in the unfortunate event of your death and paying money back in monthly sums rather than in one huge payment over a period of time. While these are great examples of hedging because you are able to see how leveraging is working on a smaller scale, the big stock market players see hedging a bit differently. To conglomerates such as the New York Stock Exchange, hedging is a bit different in the sense that it is typically used in a way that will counter the potential for competitors within an industry to cause you to lose money. Let's look at an example for this concept. Let's go out on a limb here and say that the Q-Tip industry has suddenly revolutionized itself. You are interested in getting in on this action, so you decide to invest in a company called Waxless. You think that everything is sound with your investment and you are sure that the Q-Tip industry's technology is going to skyrocket in value, only you come to find out that this "revolution" was not that great of an invention and the technology is actually causing people to have negative side effects. Due to these revelations, you come to find out that Waxless may have not been the best investment choice after all; however, you're willing to see things through a bit longer and see how the industry ends up doing in the long-term. In this situation, you are actually finding out that the Q-Tip industry is quite volatile in nature. In an attempt to counter this volatility, you decide that you're going to purchase a stock in a competing Q-Tip company that is called EarDry. EarDry has adapted the technology that Waxless initially came out with, and there is some controversy in the industry about whether the Waxless technology or the EarDry technology is superior. Because you have decided to invest in EarDry and Waxless, you are putting your investments in a good position. Rather than only investing in one type of technology within the same sector of business, you decide to put some money into both. This way, in the event that one goes under, you will still have some security in the other methods. As one falls, it's likely that the other will rise and become the superior product on the market.

Hopefully through the example above, you have a better idea of how hedging works and how you can take advantage of it for yourself. The truth is, every type of investment should have some sort of hedge to go along with it.

The real estate industry is known for its hedging tactics, as is the mortgage business as well. Let's take a look at some of the advantages that hedging can bring to the table for you, so that you can see why so many people use options in this manner.

Hedging Advantage 1: The Transfer of Risk

One of the biggest reasons why using options as a way to hedge is because of the ability for the hedge to transfer and diminish risk. Not only can hedging help to alleviate the stress that risk plays on your portfolio as a whole, but it can also serve to pacify other stressors of life as well. For example, if you're planning on opening a new business or own a home, hedging the risk that is associated with these sometimes-volatile ventures can help to bring you greater overall security.

Of course, it's certainly important to understand that hedging should not be used in a way that's going to seek to alleviate the risk that's involved with betting everything that you own, but it is a way to compliment riskier options investment behavior.

Hedging Advantage 2: The Ability to Use Forward Contracts

In addition to diminishing some of the risk that is involved in trading options and using the technique of hedging, another advantage the hedging can provide the advanced options trader is the ability to engage in forward contracts. Forward contracts are pretty similar to options in the sense that they are obviously contracts, but they are also only good for a specific period of time. Unlike options, which are typically domestic in nature, forward contracts allow an investor to trade overseas and through international currency. If you're not currently using forward contracts as a way to hedge some of the risk that's involved when trading foreign currency, it might be a good idea to consider doing so. The idea is that while it may cost more to participate in the foreign market with a forward contract, you are offsetting this cost over the long-term.

Hedging Advantage 3: Currency Declination

Lastly, another advantage that hedging can offer an options trader again deals with a situation where he or she is trading options on the foreign market. Investors who are holding options in foreign markets often run the risk of having the currency decline while the options shares are still in their possession. It's important to understand that an option that is being used in conjunction with a foreign currency will only outperform the foreign currency if the foreign currency declines in relation to the dollar. While it's certainly a good idea to consider investing in foreign currency as a way to both diversify your portfolio and use hedging to your advantage in the greatest possible manner, you have to make sure that you understand how the foreign currency is going to operate under all different types of circumstances.

CHAPTER 16:

How to Find A Broker?

Finding a suitable Brokerage account is a critical activity for any serious investor looking to trade Option in the market. Not all online brokers are suited to options trading however and some have very strict rules, which are serious constraints on a beginner's activities. Interestingly, as options are becoming more main-stream and are finally being seen as a way to manage risk and use leverage rather than a field for reckless speculation things are improving. Indeed, many brokers are beginning to welcome beginners in options trading as they now view them as serious risk-aware traders that are diversifying into options to boost their profits.

However, for the investor it is still a problem finding a suitable brokerage because it is true that any broker can buy and sell stocks, but not all of them have the skills, knowledge and the online tools to help their clients in establishing and executing options-based transactions and strategies. Nonetheless, each year more brokerages are stepping up to the plate with improved portfolios of services aimed at the options trader. So, here are some of the things that you'll want to be looking out for when you're searching for an options broker.

Tools to assess options strategies

Evaluating and selecting appropriate options involves different analysis and information than picking the underlying stocks. Picking options on that stock will require looking at measures of market conditions, bid-ask spread, implied volatility, probability, and open interest, and trading behavior in order to come up with successful strategies. The best online options brokers will have the specialist tools and analysis charts to help you evaluate which options are a good match with your trading strategy.

They will also be able to provide access to trading simulators, historical and current market data, analytical platforms, and easy to navigate quote and order functions.

A trading platform that works with your strategy

Trading options can be very complicated especially when you advance into using risk-defined combination strategies to manage and risk and limit losses. Most beginners will start out simply buying or selling single Call or Put options on a particular stock. However, as their skills and experience develop, they will gravitate towards using more advanced options strategies, which requires building a trading strategy by buying or selling combinations of different types of options. Constructing and coordinating the deployment of these strategies is very difficult unless your options broker's trading platform support these types of strategies. Ideally, they should be available as a turn-key option and selectable from a menu whereby the platform will do all the heavy-lifting in constructing these multi-leg combination orders.

The best trading platforms will have simple interfaces that make it easy to navigate and are intuitive to use so that you know exactly what you're doing. To most traders the platform is the broker so if you are comfortable with the trading experience then you will be happy with your options broker.

Make sure your broker's customer service agents know options

Although the vast amount of transactions will go solely through the broker's online trading platform, there will inevitably come a time when something goes wrong. This is when customer support becomes important as you will probably need to talk directly to a customer service agent in order to resolve your issue. This is when it becomes imperative that you speak to an experienced agent who can help resolve your issue quickly and efficiently.

Unfortunately, for many brokerage firms, options are a new service that they are entering into, and regular customer service agents aren't well trained or are not experienced enough in options to communicate and resolve issues effectively. The problem is that you cannot really evaluate a brokerage firm's customer service until you need their help and by that time it could be too late. However, if you go with a broker that specializes in options, they are more likely to have options specialists working in the customer service department that you can communicate with when you need them. It is also a very good sign if the brokerage has invested in omnichannel communication support and technology like bots and robot-advisors as that can greatly speed up the issue resolution process.

Check Commissions are Competitive

Commissions on options trading can be a thorny issue as they are often obscure and for a good reason as often, they are a lot higher than standard stock commissions. So, it's important not to assume that broker that has a good reputation for low-prices with stocks will be so generous with options. This is down to the economics as most options markets are a lot less liquid than the markets for individual stocks so there isn't the same economy of scale. Sometimes, you'll have to work with standard stock commissions and then add on an additional commission for the option. Others thankfully will just charge a one-off fee for each option transaction (2-leg). However, there are several other fees you need to be aware of with options, such as margin charges and exercise transaction fees so you will need to dig through the fine print as sometimes the fees to exercise an option can be excessive. Nonetheless, it is certainly true, that often you get what you pay for and in some cases, paying higher commissions will be worth the price if it equates to high-quality service.

Get trained on options

It is actually in the broker's interest to educate you in options trading or any financial trading for that matter. As not only will you use those services you will likely be more competent and take up less of their time trying to resolve your mistakes. However, some brokers are better than others and go a lot further than is strictly required to educate their clients in strategies, tactics and transaction processes. Most brokers will have freely available educational materials mainly online videos about options trading and these are often comprehensive catalogues covering just about every technical aspect of the business. This is in the broker's interest as it provides promotional material as well as a form of lock-in as all the demos have been performed on their own platform. Hence it may be considered a red-flag if a broker has little in the way of educational material or free demos/accounts. However, at the very minimum every brokerage is required to give you disclosure documents from the Options Clearing Commission. Education, guidance and technical support on options trading can take place on many types of media. A good combination of online videos, webinars, online FAQ and accessible customer service specialists through voice, chat and email is probably a gold standard. But remember you get what you are willing to pay for – after all a brokerage is a business as well and they cannot be expected to provide a Rolls-Royce service yet charge rock-bottom commissions. If you are willing to accept the trade-off you can get you what you need to be a more effective options investor at the price you are willing to pay. Spend time evaluating brokerages, try out their demo platforms if you can and be diligent in finding the best broker that matches your needs as getting it wrong could cost you serious money. To trade options well, you will need to have a good options broker. Then you will make the most of the opportunities that arise and that trading in options gives you.

Understanding Transaction Fees and Slippage

Broker fees across the trading world vary greatly as can be seen from the sample listed above. However, saying that they do all tend to charge fees based upon per transactions or leg (2 legs per transaction a buy and a sell) and something that they call slippage.

Slippage is the term used to account for the difference between a quoted price and the actual price you pay or are paid for a stock. In today's fast markets slippage has become unavoidable as prices change so rapidly. The amount of price slippage is determined by the difference between the bid and the asking price - the spread. The larger the spread the more likely there will be significant slippage, as it's a sign of low liquidity and volume.

There are two ways to approach minimizing slippage:

Use limit orders instead of market orders – Limit orders will only execute at the price you set, market orders on the other hand will always fill the order at the best available price and that is the primary cause of slippage.

Consider slippage to be a cost of doing business – If using limit orders is unsuitable – in many cases they are as there will be times that you must guarantee opening or closing a position – then you must calculate the likely cost of slippage into the financials.

The ways to calculate slippage - as a cost of doing business, just like all the other fees and commissions - is to use the following formula:

Amount of bid-ask spread in dollars x 100 (shares) x 1 (contract) x 2 (legs (open/close)) = slippage

CHAPTER 17:

Trading with Leaps

The acronym LEAPS stand for Long-term Equity Anticipation Securities. They are a type of option with expiration dates that are longer than normal. They last for at least 1 year and sometimes go as far as 3 years into the future. As mentioned earlier, the expiration dates of options are typically a few months into the future. The typical option expiration ranges are 3 months, 6 months and 9 months.

This is because options are typically a short-term way of investing.

LEAPS step away from the norm and have a longer shelf-life compared to your average option. They still possess the qualities as a normal option. LEAPS appeal to investors that want a long-term investment without being obliged by that investment. It also appeals to the investor who is anticipating a profitable yield from a particular market in the future but does not have the capital at hand to make that substantial investment.

They are more affordable than such assets like stock because despite the longer expiration date, they are still options and thus, stick to option price ranges. LEAPS normally have a slightly higher price than other short-term contracts

LEAPS have a seat at the options table because sometimes the value of the associated asset needs more time to appreciate in value. Typical options expire in a few months. These options can yield profits in a short amount of time but there is also the risk that the transaction might not be as profitable if the stock or other associated asset does not move significantly up or down.

LEAPS are the solution that allow that time for appreciation of the associated asset. A trader can even extend the expiration on that LEAP option with another LEAP if the time period is still too short for the asset to reach profitability. For example, a LEAP with an expiration date of 2 years can be held for 1 year then be sold to replace it with a 3-year expiration date. This is called rolled LEAPS.

Rolling the option forward is normally relatively inexpensive because it still carries the same characteristics. There are other factors that can become unpredictable, though. Such factors include interest rates, dividends and volatility.

The question that stumps many traders about LEAPS is whether to use a call option or a put option. The answer to that is dependent on whether the trader expects a bullish or bearish price movement. If the trader believes that the associated asset is bullish by the expiration date, he or she should buy call options. If instead he or she believes that the associated asset will drop in value by the expiration date, then the trader should buy put options.

Best Strategies for Using LEAPs

Some strategies work best when it pertains to LEAPS and this list includes:

Rolling LEAPS options. As mentioned earlier, this involves selling the LEAPS before expiration date while buying LEAPS with similar characteristics with at least 2-year expiration dates at the same time.

Bull call spread. This options strategy is considered to reduce the initial cost of buying a call option.

This can help offset the higher cost of LEAPS compared to standard options. Only use this strategy if you are confident that there will be a moderate rise in the price of the stock to send it up to the strike price.

Bull call spread. This is another strategy meant to offset the higher cost of LEAPs. It is a bearish strategy. Profits are earned when the stock prices fall.

Calendar call spread. This strategy is meant for a trader who wishes to benefit from the associated assets staying stagnant in the market while also benefiting from the long-term call position if the stock becomes more valuable in the future.

The Benefits of LEAPS

LEAPS have several benefits and they include:

LEAPS are sustainable as they allow a trader to piggyback off market trends. This allows the trader to observe the movement of stock prices and have an option to buy or sell without making the full commitment of ownership.

LEAPS are less volatility and so offer greater security. A trader who enters into such an option is looking at a stock that is increasing or decreasing in price over the long haul. This allows the trader the time to really ponder on the profitability of pursuing the asset. This person can use data offered over that time such as the current trends, news and terms to base their future decision.

LEAPS can serve a great security in your financial portfolio as well as provide shareholders with a greater grip of the stock.

LEAPS allow time for improvisation because the expiration date is longer.

Buying LEAPS is cheaper than buying several standard options back to back.

The Disadvantages of LEAPS

There are two sides to every coin. So, just as LEAPS are beneficial, there are also a few downsides. The first disadvantage of LEAPS is the strike price. Because they are priced higher, the trader needs to see movement in the asset price to gain a profit in addition to it taking longer for the option holder to breakeven.

The longer expiration dates on LEAPS make them less predictable. Therefore, pricing correctly so that a return is seen without the transaction being too costly is made can be difficult. Lastly, the trader will not benefit from any attached dividends or stock repurchase.

LEAPS are also sensitive to implied volatility and so, can lower in value when implied volatility drops.

Tips for Getting the Most Out Of LEAPS

Pretend as if you are actually investing. This allows you to search for assets that you are actually interested in and maybe already have some know-how about. This makes it a lot easier to keep up-to-date with market trends compared to if you do not know anything about the asset and are not interested in learning more.

Make use of the long expiration date. The benefits of the longer expiration date have been stated so ensure that these work to your benefit.

Choose LEAPS that are more liquid.

Prepare for the fact that LEAPS are more volatile than stocks but less volatile than standard options.

Set targets for the stock prices in comparison to your LEAPS. Knowing those targets will allow the trader to sell at the most profitable time.

Have an exit strategy in case the option is not working out according to plan.

Always be aware of your position and be prepared to leverage it. Even though the expiration date is far off, you need to keep abreast as to whether the market is playing out as you anticipated. You need to be aware of the fluctuations in the asset's price. This will allow you to make a determination that makes this transaction the most profitable it can be for you. You can implement strategies like rolling the option forward and selling the first option as a loss so that you can move to another strike price that benefits you more.

CHAPTER 18:

Options Greeks

G reeks are five parameters denoted by Greek symbols (or letters) that quantify the way the price of an option will change. You don't have to know how they work precisely, only what they mean. At any given time, you can look them up to get their values. We start by looking at intrinsic value, that is, how the price of the option changes or varies with the underlying stock's price.

Delta

If you look at the data for any option, you are going to see five Greek letters (usually expressed by their English spelled names) delta, theta, gamma, vega, and rho. The first of these is delta, which tells you how the price of an option changes with the price of the underlying stock.

We noted earlier that the price of an option doesn't have a 1-1 change in price in relation to the stock. You can see exactly how it will change by looking at delta. First, we'll consider call options. So, if delta is 0.46, that means if the underlying stock price rises by $1, the price of the option is going to increase by $0.46. If delta were 0.74, then the price of the option would rise by $0.74 if the price of the underlying stock went up by $1.

Put options have a negative delta, which just indicates that a put option has an inverse relationship to the price of the underlying stock. That is if the price of the underlying stock goes down, the value of a put option goes up, and if the price of the underlying stock goes up, the value of the put option goes down.

So, if delta is -0.26, and the price of the underlying stock went up by $1, the value of the put option would drop by 26 cents. On the other hand, if the price of the underlying stock had dropped by $1, then the price of the put option would rise by $0.26.

Delta is dynamic, and the number always changes when some important parameter in the options price changes. Consider an option on a stock that is trading at $102 with a strike price of $100, with 14 days to option expiration. In this case, the price of the call option is $2.48, and delta is 0.75. The price of the put option is $0.47, and delta for the put option is -0.25. So, if the price of the underlying stock goes up by $1, we expect the call option to rise to $2.48 + $0.75 = $3.23. The price of the put option would decrease to $0.47 - $0.25 = $0.22.

That's just about what happens, but in reality, the relationship isn't quite exact since other things impact the price of the options. The call option increases to $3.84, and the put option declines in price to $0.27.

We said its dynamic, and what happens when the share price rises by $1, is the delta values for both options change as well. Now delta is 0.84 for the call, and -0.16 for the put.

That tells us something important, namely that delta is higher the more in the money the stock is. We can see this looking at some real options. Considering an IBM $124 call that expires on 6/28, it has a delta of 0.967. A $139 call that expires on 6/28 has a delta of 0.5388. The share price is $139.20, so the $124 call is more in the money. The $139 call is practically at the money, and we learn a second important fact about delta, that is that at the money options will have a delta that is reasonably close to 0.50.

Since the more in the money you are, the higher delta, that means in the money options can benefit (or be hurt by) a $1 change in the price of the underlying stock.

Something else that happens is that if the option is in the money, the closer you get to expiration, the higher delta goes. For our example of an option with a $100 share price, if the underlying stock price remains at $103, moving to 7 days from expiration, delta jumps to 0.92 for the call. Moving to 3 days to expiration, delta is 0.98. So, if you are expecting a stock price to move a lot in the following few days, getting an option that will expire soon before the move happens could be a worthwhile investment. Look for events that could impact the price, such as earnings call or product announcement.

If an option is out of the money, the closer to the expiration date, you get the smaller delta gets. In fact, a few days away from expiration delta can get vanishingly small. An out of the money call option for a strike price of $100, share price of $97 with three days to expiration will have a delta of 0.02.

The delta for the same put option will add up the difference to 100 (but remember it's expressed as a negative value). In this case, a put option with the same parameters, so a strike price of $100 – will have a delta of -0.98 if the underlying price is $97. In that case, the put would be worth $3.00, and if the underlying share price dropped to $96, the price of the put would rise to $4. Then you'd see delta increase to -1.00 for the put and drop to 0.00 for the call.

If the stock had moved the other way, risen in price by $1, then delta for the put would drop to -0.92 instead, and the price of the put would drop to $2.04. The bottom line is delta will give you a good estimate of how much the price of the option will change when the price of the underlying stock changes by $1. If it's a call option, the relationship is direct, and delta is expressed as a positive number. For put options, since the relationship is an inverse one, delta is a negative number. And remember that if you take the absolute value of delta for the put option and add it to the delta value for a call option that has the same strike value and date of expiration, they will sum to 1.0.

Gamma

Gamma is like the second derivative. In other words, it tells you how delta itself changes. This is important since we noted that delta was dynamic. However, beginning traders don't need to dive into this too deeply, but you can check gamma to see about how much delta will change if there is a $1 change in the price of the underlying shares. Gamma has the same value for both puts and calls. So if Gamma were 0.22 and delta was 0.24 for a call option, and -0.76 for a put option with the same strike and expiration date, we'd expect a $1 rise in share price to cause delta for the call option to increase to 0.46, and the delta for the put option would change to -0.54. That is about what would happen, but remember if the option were at the money the values of delta would move to 0.5 and -0.5, respectively.

Theta

When examining options, theta is a very important parameter among the Greeks. What theta gives you information about is the time decay of the option. Theta is expressed as a negative number, reflecting the fact that time decay causes a decrease in option price as time goes on. Let's consider a couple of examples. Suppose that we have call and put options with a strike price of $100 with three days to expiration. The price of the call is $1.20, and the price of the put is $0.20 if the share price of the underlying stock is $101. In this case, theta is -0.073 for both the call and the put. That tells us that if nothing else changes, the price of each option will decrease by $0.073. The call option is priced at $1.20, and the put is priced at $0.20. Moving to 2 days to expiration and leaving everything else the same, we find that the price of the call option drops to $1.12, and the price of the put option drops to $0.12, so it moved in almost exact accordance to what was expected. The following day theta has increased to -0.079, reflecting the fact that time decay happens more rapidly the closer you get to the expiration date of the option. In fact, with everything else unchanged, 20 days to expiration theta is about half as strong, at -0.035. That reflects one of the fundamental truths of options, that is that time decay happens in an exponential fashion, with time decay happening faster the closer you get to expiration.

One of the things that help make options seem complicated is that all of these variables are interdependent. So, at 20 days to expiration, suppose the stock price shot up to $108. In that case, theta decreases to -0.005. So, it's only 1/7th of the earlier value. It decreases for the put option as well. Theta is also proportional to share price. So, theta is larger if the share price is larger. Consider a stock with a share price of $975, and a strike price of $1,000. In that case, theta is -0.282 for the call option and -0.274 for the put option. That means if a day passes and nothing else changes, the value of the call option (which in this case is $5.15) will drop by about $0.28, and the value of the put option will drop by about $0.27. The fundamental lesson here is the same as it was beforehand, that time decay is an important fundamental when it comes to options pricing. Check the Greek theta to get an idea of how the price of the option is going to decay by the following day if all other things are held equal.

Vega

The following Greek that we are going to meet is Vega, which tells us the relationship between the price of the option and the implied volatility. What Vega tells you is how sensitive the option is to changes in the implied volatility. Generally speaking, an in the money option is less sensitive to changes in implied volatility, while an out of the money option is more sensitive to changes in implied volatility. Specifically, vega tells you how much the price of the option will change if the implied volatility changes by 1%. Remember that options that have higher implied volatility are worth more money.

When you are in long positions, vega is positive, and it's negative for short positions.

Rho

Rho is a measure of the options pricing's sensitivity to a change in the risk-free interest rate. Since interest rates don't change by that much or that often these days, rho isn't paid much attention to. In a radically changing high-interest rate environment such as existed in the late 1970s, rho would be a more important parameter to pay attention to.

CHAPTER 19:

Candlestick Charts

A candlestick chart is a method of plotting financial data that tells you how prices moved over a given trading session. Rather than having a continuous curve, the price data is broken down into different time frames. There is not a specific time frame that is used; you can create candlestick charts using various time frames. For example, you can have a chart break up a trading day into fifteen-minute increments. Then, the candlesticks will be created for each fifteen-minute increment throughout each trading day, and it will give you pricing information for each of those increments. You can break prices down by the minute, by five-minutes, by an hour, by four hours, and so on. When you are looking for the right time to enter and exit trades once you have decided that it is about the right time to do so, you might use one minute or five-minute intervals. This will also depend on how active trading is. If a stock is moving by a lot, over the course of a few minutes, options prices can change drastically. So if you have a call option on Netflix in your portfolio, and you are looking to sell it, if prices of the underlying stock are moving by a significant amount, you are going to want to keep close tabs on short term pricing changes, and so you might use a five-minute candlestick chart for this purpose.

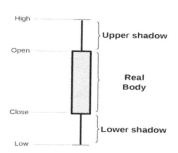

Candlestick charts are quite general in their application. They can be used for any financial asset that is traded in real-time. In fact, they were originally developed in Japan, to track changes in the price of rice. So, they can be used for commodities, stocks, bonds, Forex, or any other asset. Naturally, they are used for stocks, which is why we are discussing them, and our discussion will be focused on that.

Looking at the basic unit of a candlestick chart, which is a trading session of the selected time length, the first thing to look at is the color. At a glance, the color of a candlestick tells you the direction of price movement in that trading session. There are different color schemes used on charts, but for stocks, it is typical to use a white background. If the price of the stock went up over the time period, then the color is going to be green. If the price of the stock dropped over the time period, the color is going to be red.

The candlestick is going to have a "body" and "wicks" coming out of it (in some treatments, the wicks are referred to as "shadows"). The length of the body tells you how much the price moved over the course of the entire trading session. This information is to be taken in conjunction with the color of the candlestick.

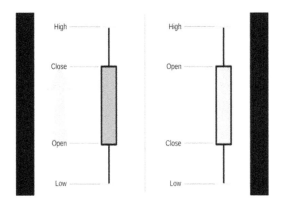

If the candlestick is green, then the bottom of the candlestick is the opening price for the trading session (low in value), and the top of the candlestick is the closing price of the trading session (high in value – so the price rose over the trading session).

119

If the candlestick is red, the relationships are reversed. In this case, the top of the candlestick is the opening price for the trading session. Then, the bottom of the candlestick is going to be the lower, closing price of the trading session, reflecting that the stock lost value over the time period.

Red and green candlesticks are also referred to by the mood they represent. If a candlestick is red, the mood is "bearish" since people are getting out of the stock, and so it can be referred to as a bearish candlestick. Conversely, if the mood is bullish, prices are rising, and people are trying to buy into the stock, and so, a green candlestick is bullish.

The wicks on a candlestick have the same meaning regardless of color. The top wick is the high price attained during the trading session, and the bottom wick is the low price seen during the trading session.

Candlesticks can help you determine the momentum of trading. If the wicks are long, but the body is short, that helps you determine that there was a large push of the price in one direction or another, but there was not enough momentum to sustain it, and prices ended up moving back to where they were when the trading session opened, or at least relatively close by. Remember that pricing is related to supply and demand. So, if prices are rising, there is more demand for the stock. If prices are dropping, people are dumping the stock (increasing the supply), and demand is decreasing.

Candlesticks and Trends

The main way that candlesticks are used is to spot changes in price trends. So, you want to be paying close attention to candlesticks when the stock price has been dropping or rising for a period of time, and you are looking for signals that a reversal in the price trend is about to occur.

A sudden shift from selling to buying or vice versa is one way that a trend reversal can be noted. This is indicated by an "enveloping" candlestick. That is, you have a candlestick of one type that is larger than the preceding candlestick of the opposite type, then you have a situation where a trend reversal is indicated.

Take, for example, the situation where stock prices have been declining. You are going to see some fluctuation, but there is going to be largely a trend of red candlesticks reflecting the trend of dropping prices. When you see a small red candlestick followed by a bullish candlestick that has a body that is large enough to completely engulf the body of the bearish or red candlestick that preceded it, this is usually a sign that the sell-off is over, and prices are going to start rising. So, this is an indication that you want to buy a call option (or sell a put option) on the stock at this point. When prices are rising, you look for a bearish candlestick to engulf a bullish candlestick to indicate that peak price has been reached, and people are going to start selling off the stock.

Another indicator of a change in trend is when you have seen a trend in one direction, and then you see three candlesticks in a row of the opposite type. Let's consider a downward trend in prices first. If prices have been dropping, then you see three green or bullish candlesticks in a row, particularly when each succeeding candlestick has a higher closing price, this is a solid indication that prices are going to reverse, and the stock is entering an upward price trend. On the other hand, if you are at the top of an uptrend, and you see three bearish candlesticks in a row, each with lower closing prices than the preceding candlestick, that tells you that the stock price is probably going to start dropping.

Of course, these are rules of thumb; they are not exact or guaranteed to lead to the results described. They often or usually do, but you should confirm these signals using another tool before making major trading decisions.

A "hammer" is another important signal to look for. A hammer is a candlestick that has a narrow body, and one wick that sticks out for either from the top or bottom, with no wick on the opposite side (or at least a wick on the opposite side that is comparatively smaller). A hammer can be inverted, with the wick sticking out from the top, or just a hammer, with the wick sticking out from the bottom. In either case, this represents a case of prices being pushed one way, but then there was a complete momentum shift that prevented that from having a lasting impact.

If you are at the bottom of a downtrend and prices were pushed downward by a large degree during the trading session, but then they end up rising high enough so that the price closes higher than the opening, this is a bullish hammer. It could be an indication that the downward trend of prices has come to an end, and momentum has shifted. You can look for a similar signal with an inverted hammer that is bearish at the top of an uptrend. This would indicate that prices were again pushed up during the trading session, but then momentum reversed, causing prices to drop and end up lower than the opening of the session, indicating that the mood has become bearish and people are beginning to sell off their stocks.

Moving Averages

There are many more signals that you can get from candlestick charts, but the most potent technical indicator that can be used to detect price trend reversals is the moving average. A stock market chart is very jagged in appearance because of the volatility that we conferred earlier. However, a lot of the price movements are nothing more than noise. It would be nice to smooth out the data to eliminate that noise so that we could get a smooth curve that represents the actual underlying price movement of the asset. This can be done, and it is done by averaging the prices of the stock over a given time period.

By taking the average of a given number of past time periods together, and calculating it at each point along the line, we can generate what is called a moving average. You can have a simple moving average, which just gives you the straightforward arithmetic average of the prices used. Or you can use other moving averages that weight prices, giving more weight to recent prices as opposed to earlier prices. The most popular weighted moving average is the exponential moving average.

The way that moving averages are used on a stock chart is to have two moving averages shown together. The period of the moving average is the number of trading sessions that are averaged together. So, a 9-period moving average will use the past nine closing prices to determine the average at each point, while a 20-period moving average is going to use the past twenty closing prices to compute the average.

To use moving averages to detect price trend reversals, a longer period moving average is plotted together with a short period moving average. The trader then looks for cross overs of the short period moving average with respect to the long period moving average in order to detect reversals in the price trend. There are no hard rules about what periods to use, but many traders use nine-period moving averages with twenty period moving averages, and some use fifty-period moving averages together with 200-period moving averages.

If the short period moving average moves above the long period moving average, this is a strong indicator that there is going to be a trend of increasing prices. For this reason, this type of crossing is referred to as a golden cross in the day trading community. You can check the candlesticks when you have seen this type of signal to see if the candlesticks are showing a pattern that would confirm an increasing trend in prices is coming. When both of them agree, this is a good indication that you are seeing a real change in the underlying trend.

CHAPTER 20:

Pros of Trading Equities

1. Equities have significantly high liquidity.

Compared to options markets, equity markets are significantly more liquid. For most traders and investors, it is easy to enter and exit positions. This can happen within minutes in most cases. Exiting positions within a matter of a few minutes is especially easy for stocks that constitute major indexes such as the S&P 500. This liquidity often comes from mutual funds and passive index funds that are invested in the S&P 500 stocks. These funds are regularly seeking to invest in stocks contained in the fund in order to own larger percentages.

2. Time is on your side.

Options give you very little time to profit from market movements. This is not the case when it comes to stocks. In fact, stocks have no time limit which means you can hold them for as long as you see necessary.

As a stock investor, you have plenty of time within which you can enter and exit trades.

You will not be punished for early or late entry into trades. However, options traders really need to factor in time because options contracts are limited by time.

3. Stocks generally have a lower risk.

Both stocks and options have their own pros and cons. However, in general, traders and investors view stocks as being generally less risky. The volatility of any given stock is generally much lower than that of options. Also, stocks have no risks due to time decay.

Disadvantages Associated with Stocks

There are certain downsides of equities trade compared to options contracts. We will examine some of these disadvantages and see how they compare to options.

1. Stocks have limited upside.

Most stocks move in tandem with respective indexes. Stocks rarely move above 20% in any given year. Traders with limited finances or small capital will be frustrated to discover that even with all the time in the world, their income potential is limited. This contrasts traders who focus on other instruments such as options who are able to double their income in just a few short months or even weeks. Just a few well-managed options trade and good risk management techniques, it is very possible for multiple investments within a short time period.

2. Stocks have limited leverage.

Investors in stocks can only access limited capital through borrowing of only up to 50% of the total value of securities they have purchased. This refers to margin loans that are advanced by brokerage firms to clients.

This limitation is placed by the federal government through the Federal Reserve's regulations. This regulation applies only to equities markets but not the derivatives markets. The use of excessive leverage is discouraged and generally frowned upon. However, investors with capital amounts totaling about $5,000 can access marginal loans of up to $10,000 which they can use to invest in trades.

3. Higher risks for lower profits.

It is possible to put money in a stock and actually lose the entire amount. While this is very rare and hardly occurs, it can happen should the asset's value tumble down to zero. When it comes to options, you only stand to lose your initial investment only which in most cases is the premium paid for the options contract.

While the losses may sound similar in both cases, this is not so. The amount of capital needed to invest in stocks is vastly different from amounts used in options trading.

Other Crucial Considerations

In order to make informed decisions about whether to buy, sell, or hold stocks, you need to understand more about a company's operations and business. You also need to understand the company's vision and have a sense of direction where the asset is heading. This is crucial, especially for options traders.

To be successful, options investors should have an excellent understanding of a company's intrinsic value and also affirm thesis regarding the foundations of a business and how near-term events will affect its performance such as macroeconomics. Numerous investors can choose to think options just add complexity to their basket of investments. However, if you really want to earn big profits and enjoy attractive returns on your investments, then options trading and investments is really the way to go. It is crucial that you learn how to trade options and how to limit your downsides.

Choosing Options Over Stocks

Leverage

When you buy options, your potential gains are virtually unlimited while any potential losses are limited to your original investment and any additional costs incurred such as the brokerage fees. Therefore, in theory, your potential gains are limitless while losses are capped to the amount paid as premium.

Also, you spend significantly less to invest in stocks through options compared to direct stocks investments. For instance, to buy $10,000 worth of stocks, you will need to fork out at least that much money. With options, you will pay a tiny fraction of this amount. However, you stand to gain the same returns in both cases.

Fine-tuning Strategies

When you invest your funds in shares, your options are pretty much limited to buying or selling shares. However, with options, it is easy to identify a strategy that does fit your expectations. Stock options can be purchased and exercised in numerous combinations that enable traders to fine-tune strategies so that they can match market conditions whether bearish, bullish, neutral or in-between.

For example, as an options investor, you can opt to select a variety of expiration dates. These can range between about-to-expire monthly options with LEAPS that have close to three years before expiration. It is possible to find a strike that is based on both your risk tolerance and stock performance expectation.

With this approach, you are also able to benefit significantly from high market volatility simply by choosing a strategy that will benefit you from major movements in either direction like the short straddle. Options are also widely used for hedging positions such as the protective put and for managing risk such as with the stock replacement strategy.

CHAPTER 21:

Stock Investing Trading Strategies for Beginners

Strategies for Investing in stocks

Stock trading needs a lot of understanding to stay in the trade and get the anticipated profits. The use of different strategies in stock trading helps the traders know when to invest and how to invest. The following strategies will help investors in trading with the stocks.

Value investing

Value investing strategy is an easy but yet hard strategy that traders employ. Most of the traders go for the stocks that they are unable to sell ultimately. In this strategy, the traders buy the undervalued stocks of the company. Experienced traders can smoothly go about this because they understand it well. They will buy stocks from the profiting companies that other traders think is undervalued when compared to the current market prices. The traders then wait until when the prices the market price moves to make their gains. The new traders in stock trading with limited knowledge about stocks may go for the wring stocks. They may go for the undervalued stocks, yes, but from a company that is not making a profit in the market. This gives a trade a hard time to sell the stocks.

When you use the value investing strategy for a long time, you will realize that it is more involving than you thought before. It is always good to control your psychology when using this strategy. The emotional torment of greed overpowers most traders employing this strategy. They all of a sudden, realize that they need more money faster because the undervalued stocks picked up the prices and gave them good returns. Most traders here decide to buy more underestimated stock believing that they will get more returns faster. This is an unsafe move because the prices may not even change, thus causing them significant losses. It is always good to be wise when employing this strategy. The traders using this strategy are advised to purchase their stocks from reliable companies that maintain their success.

Growth Stock investment Strategy

Traders using this strategy aim at increasing their capital. The traders invest in growth stocks. They buy stocks from a small company that they have analyzed and seen the potential of growth in prices of their stocks. This strategy works very well if well analyzed. Buying stocks from a young company can bring excellent returns when the markets are favorable. Most traders using this strategy in stocks get huge profits but are exposed to high risks because the young companies have not been tried, and therefore anything can happen. The prices may not turn out as expected in the market hence incurring losses.

There are no specific companies that the growth investors go for stocks. They can look for the stocks even in the whole market as long as they find what is suitable. The traders using this strategy mostly go for the stocks in stock companies that are growing faster. They consider the technologies being used in those companies, the profits in the companies and then evaluate the gains they will get if they buy the stocks and sell. These traders also compare the dividends they will earn when they become stock owners.

The Fusion of Growth and Value Investing

Fusion investing is the investment by traders while combining the fundamental, technical and behavioral analysis without looking at the historical background of the stocks. The feelings of the investor and the underlying value of the trade are assimilated. Fusion Growth and value investing strategy, valuation analysis is done by a trader through calculations to help in the prediction of the future stock value. Through his calculations, he will look at the cash flow discounts offered in the trade of the stocks and use them to calculate the present value. The present value calculated will help in the future prediction of trade of the stocks.

A trader who does not calculate the present value of the stocks is likely to be carried away during the trade. He will overtrade or go for the wrong stocks that will come tumbling down. Most noise traders lose because they are carried away by a slight show of a win. They invest without valuing the stocks and in the end; they will incur enormous losses that will handicap them trade wisely.

In this investment strategy, the trader chooses shares from a share populace (group) that he believes have value. From the populace, the shares that the trader believes are more critical are chosen. Lastly, he selects the stocks that he believes to have the potential to continue moving in the required direction. These are the shares that have momentum. Selection of shares from share population and the selection of the fundamental share by the trader are made yearly, while the selection of the shares that have momentum is made monthly. This strategy tries to combine the traditional and behavioral models to get a powerful investment model.

Passive Index Investing

Passive index investing strategy is also called the buy-and-hold approach. The investors using these strategies invest their money in different stocks with the expectations of getting higher returns as per the investment. The investors here do not aim at benefiting quickly from the short-term trades. They buy their stocks and hold. The traders believe that you can never know more than what the market holds. You cannot think smarter than the market itself.

Traders applying this strategy assimilate with the market trend. They do not sell their stocks or buy them before or after the market shows the potential to sell or buy characteristics. The investors here hold their stocks to limit the fees applicable to them during frequent trading. The main aim of passive investors is to make the profits widely. They are comfortable withholding on their stocks because they believe that the market's returns become positive over a long period.

Indicators of Investing Stock Strategies

There are different indicators of stocks that will help a trader understand the direction of the stock in the market and how to trade. Most traders use technical indicators so as they can get profits in a short period. Nonetheless, these technical indicators used by short term traders are also useful and vital to the long-term traders. Different technical indicators are used when trading in the stock. The types of indicators used while stock trading is;

● Trend indicators. These indicators show the direction in which the market is moving. It shows when the market is taking a downward trend, and an upward trend or a sideways trend.

● Volatility Indicators. These indicators focus on the uncertainty in the market. The measure of this uncertainty is in standard deviation.

● The volume indicators. These indicators are good at showing the signals. They can point out any break out in the trend line or the crossing of the moving signals when they are in company in the market.

The indicators below help the trader understand what to do in stock trading;

Simple Moving Averages

The simple moving averages also denotes as SMA, are trend indicators. They show the direction the stocks are taking in the stock market. Simple moving averages indicator is convenient to use, and it is easy to calculate. When an analyst is computing using this indicator, he takes the simple averages of the closing stock of a specified period. Most short-term traders use 10- day prices of stocks to calculate the SMA while the long-term traders use the 100-day price or the 200-day prices in their computations. A signal is thrown in when the stock prices remain above for an extended period. The markets bully the stocks, and that is why it is called the bullish.

While using the simple moving averages indicator, the traders are advised to be very keen when making their entry or exit. A trader should make his purchase when the prices are going up and approaching the long-term moving average. This will give him good prices when the selling time comes. A trader should also make sure that he sells his stocks when the prices start falling under the long-term moving average. When the indicator starts showing that the prices are moving towards the long-term indicator from the bottom, the trader can make a sell. But if the indicator shows that the prices have passed the long-term moving average, the trader can now purchase his stock. For example

AZ Company's stocks for over five periods are;

$22.80. $25.30, $26.70, $25.40 and $27.70.

The SMA here = ({$22.80+25.30+26.70+25.40+27.70}/5)

=$ 25.58

The closing stocks of AZ Company are;

$30.00, $25.30, $25.60, $24.50 and $27.50.

SMA =$26.25.

We have seen that long-term trade has more days; this means this calculation can continue until you finish all the periods that you want to calculate.

Rate of Change

It is denoted as ROC. This indicator shows the momentum of the prices in the stock market. It shows how stock prices keep developing. The prices can take a different momentum depending on the market. Traders use a 14-day time frame to calculate the rate of change in the prices. Two percentages of varying periods are arrived at and compared to each other. The positive rate of change shows an entry signal in this indicator. It shows the prices will turn and pick the required trend. Traders can make their entry in the trade when this signal appears. A warning signal is flushed when the prices start going up while the rate of change remains the same. This trend is a signal that a reversal is on the way, and traders should make their exit.

RSI-RELATIVE STRENGTH INDEX

Right from its name, the relative strength index indicator shows the strength of the prices of the stocks in the market. Relative Strength Index analyzes prices as overbought and ready for collection when the indicator is above 70 and looks at prices as oversold and ready to bounce when the indicator is below 30. When the stock prices are 70 or above for a certain period or duration, it indicates the trend is up, however, when the prices are 30 or below, this sets an alarm of a downward trend. Traders should buy when prices are near oversold condition because the price is going up and the traders should sell near the overbought when the price is going down.

There is no fixed timing or surety for stock trading when this indicator is used. In long term stocks trade, a buy signal appears when the Relative Strength Index moves above 50 then reverse back. This shows a pullback in prices; therefore, a trader cannot buy until the end of the withdrawal. The time a pullback ends and the trend of prices is picked again, and a trader can now purchase the stocks. When the prices are moving in an upward direction, that's an uptrend, the Relative Strength Index is always less than 30 that is why a 50 is in preference. When the indicator shows the RSI move to 30 or below, traders should watch out because a significant reversal is coming. When the RSI goes beyond 50 and then back, it is safe and short-term traders can now trade.

CHAPTER 22:

Passive Income

There are, broadly speaking, two ways of making money. The first is to exchange your time for money and the second is to exchange your money for money. The first way is to undertake something like a job or to freelance. You're investing your time into a project and in return you get paid. Yes, you're really getting paid for a result if you're freelancing but my point is that it takes time to produce that result.

The more time you spend on such tasks, the more your earning ability is. If you're a freelance writer, for example, the greater the number of high-quality words you produce, the more you're going to get paid per month. Thus, one of the important things to note about this sort of income is that when you go to sleep, so does your income stream. When asked about one of the key things that rich people do that poor people don't, Bill Gates responded by saying that the rich leverage their time a lot better (Bodnar, 2017). What does leverage time mean? Well, Gates' point was that the only thing that is truly limited in our lives is time. We cannot get back the time we've lost, no matter how much we would like to believe that time machines exist. So ultimately, being financially successful comes down to how well you manage your time. The fact of the matter is that a rich person manages to get paid more for a unit of their time than a poor person does. So how do you get paid more per hour?

Leveraging Time

One easy way is to upskill yourself. Simply learn a higher skill and work in a more lucrative field. However, even this doesn't fully leverage your time since once you go to sleep, your money tap is switched off. Hence, the thing to do is to create multiple streams of income. If you have two streams of income paying you at the same time, you can double your hourly wage.

The problem is that you can only do so much at once. You can't perform two jobs at the same moment of time. So, what you really want is another source of income that doesn't place demands on your time which will detract you from your job or hourly source of money. This is precisely what a passive income stream is.

Passive streams leverage your time by simply providing you with an additional amount of money for no additional input of time. I want to make something clear at this point; you will need to spend time creating and maintaining the passive income stream. My point is that your earning ability with this stream doesn't directly depend on how many hours you put into it.

If you spend five hours writing, you're going to get paid for the words you produced in those five hours. If you spend five hours on a passive income stream, you're not going to get paid for those five hours necessarily. You could get paid less, you could get paid more, who knows? The point is that whatever comes, adds to your income as long as you spend the time to do things correctly.

For example, a savings account provides you with passive income. A real estate investment on which you earn rent provides you with passive income. You can spend ten hours a day maintaining your property or spend two hours, it doesn't matter. It will earn you the market level of rent as long as things are maintained properly. There is an aspect of marginal utility with passive income, as economists call it (Bloomenthal, 2019).

Marginal utility refers to the return you receive, in satisfaction or dollars, for every unit of work spent. So, if you spend five hours fixing the taps, that is probably going to make you good money. Spending an additional hour figuring out which exact shade of white the walls need to be painted with is probably not going to make you much. Hence, the marginal utility of the former is a lot higher than the latter.

All passive income streams have a level of maximum marginal utility before the returns start dropping off. Trading options, if you're catching on, is subject to the same forces. Remember that your return is measured not just in money but also in the satisfaction and quality of life you receive. So, you need to figure out this value first.

A good way of understanding the value you'll receive and checking which style of trading you wish to adopt is to understand the styles of trading themselves. This way, you can make an accurate judgment of what suits you best.

Active and Passive Trading

As far as the SEC is concerned, all trading is active. Passive actions are reserved for the investment world. Whatever the good folk of the SEC might think, in reality, there are active forms of trading as well as passive forms. The diversity of the markets means that there exist many ways in which you can divide trading activity. Active versus passive simply happens to be one method of doing so.

Active trading refers to what you think traders actually do. This is where people sit glued to their terminals waiting on tenterhooks for news items to be released and then acting like hotshots when they make money. All of this is accurate except for that last bit which is a caricature. Either way, active trading usually involves taking directional bets on the market and usually hedging that with some other financial instrument.

Institutional traders, the kinds that trade for hedge funds, big banks and proprietary trading firms (prop shops), are all active traders. No matter what sort of strategies they employ and no matter which instruments they trade, they're always in touch with the markets. They need to be this way because their objective is to squeeze every ounce of money available.

In order to do so, they have to follow the market's every move. They need to know the market backwards and cannot have things sneak up on them. What's more, they need to deal with unexpected things that happen over holidays or weekends. For example, as of this writing, oil traders around the world have had to deal with the repercussions of a couple of Saudi Arabian oil fields being attacked.

This happened over the weekend and when the markets were closed. As they returned to work on Monday, you can bet that none of them had slept through the weekend. Active traders tend to look at this sort of thing as an opportunity. Market mispricing happen during such events and opportunities present themselves. One needs to love the adrenaline rush that occurs during such times. It's no surprise then, that at big banks, the average trader spends about five years on a desk before moving onto a managerial position where they supervise other traders who ultimately place all the bets.

It just isn't easy keeping up with such a lifestyle, after all. In contrast to this active trader, we have the passive trader. The passive trader's returns are not comparable to the active one's. This doesn't mean they make less money, just that they make less than the average active trader.

The tradeoff is that they get to spend their time doing something else. Understandably, a lot of big banks look down upon this sort of thing since a good quality of life on the trading desk usually means losses. However, some hedge funds and other private institutions welcome this sort of thing actively.

You see, a holy grail in the financial world is the pursuit of market neutral returns. Market neutral means that the strategy makes money no matter what the market does. In such strategies, a trader sets things up via complex financial instruments and then lets the market play itself out. This doesn't mean they go to sleep after this, they simply recycle the strategy in as many markets as possible.

Thus, while the strategy is passive the trader is active by choice in such institutions. There are some traders who fix their level of activity within prop shops by trading this way. There is a lot of freedom in such strategies since the trader is not chained to their desk out of necessity. They can vary their involvement in the market and while the returns don't compare to active strategies, the overall payoff is worth it to the trader.

Almost every passive strategy involves the use of options. The ones that don't involve the usage of derivatives that behave like options.

Pros and Cons of Passive Income

While there seem to be a lot of positives from passive income, I must warn you that it isn't all a bed of roses. Even roses have thorns, after all. The negatives that lend themselves to passive income almost entirely have to do with how people approach it. A lot of people think that this is lazy money and that things run on autopilot.

Well, this is not the case at all. Every passive income stream, including the ones to do with trading require investment of either time or money or both. In the case of passive trading income, you need to invest both. Time is needed to learn and study the markets and to develop your skills.

The markets are not easily deciphered mainly because they are chaotic. Our brains are designed to handle linear environments and understand step by step patterns easily. However, patterns that present themselves intermittently, rhyming with one another instead of replicating themselves exactly, are an alien language.

Thankfully, our brains are learning machines and over time, we can learn to spot such patterns. This is really what trading is all about. Time is needed to train your brain to get used to this new world where everything happens at random but plays out according to a perfectly predictable bigger picture.

Therefore, you need to spend time learning the markets and understanding the ins and outs of options. You need to learn their characteristics to such an extent that you should instantly be able to decide whether to adjust a trade or not. Options trades are complex on the surface since they involve at least two legs. Adjustment is a case of removing both legs or just one and establishing another leg elsewhere.

This calls for mental agility, so you need to spend time to work up to this level. Do not expect to be able to do this overnight. The other thing to invest into this is money. This is simple enough to understand.

CHAPTER 23:

Volatility

There's one final factor that affects the prices of contracts on a fundamental basis, though it's not really something we've touched on so far. The volatility of a contract is, however, an incredibly important concept to grasp for an options trader.

Volatility refers to the movement of the underlying stock. Some stocks will slowly wend their way up and down in a predictable manner – those are not very volatile. Others change on a day to day basis and change between up and down along the way.

To sum up the effect of volatility in a single sentence: the more volatile the stock, the more that an options trader is willing to pay for it. A volatile stock has a better chance of reaching the strike price and perhaps shooting far beyond it before the expiration date.

However, it's also the most dangerous of the factors that you need to bear in mind because it's arguably the most likely one to force you into a bad decision. A volatile stock, for example, can lead to a much higher premium and therefore a higher contract price; unless that stock shoots through the roof, you could actually end up losing money even when you should be making it.

One way to estimate the volatility of a stock is to take a look at what it has done in the recent past. This tells you how much it has moved up and down already, which some use as an indicator of how much it will move up and down in the future.

Unfortunately, it's not always true that the past repeats itself and you can't predict the future based on what's already happened. Instead, options traders use "implied volatility" to make their guesses: the value that the market believes the option is worth.

You can see this reflected in the activity on the options for that stock. Buyers will be keen to get their hands-on options before a certain event takes place, such as the announcement of a new product or a release about the company's earnings. Because of this, options increase in price because there is implied volatility – the market thinks the stock is going to shoot up.

You'll see lower demand on a stock that's flat or moving gently, because there is no implied volatility and therefore no hurry to get in on the action. You'll also see correspondingly low prices for the option.

Volatility is obviously a good thing – as a buyer, you want the stock to be volatile, because you need it to climb to the strike price and beyond. However, there is also such a thing as too much volatility. It's at that point the contracts become popular, the prices rise and you stand to pay more for a contract than you will ultimately profit.

Your brokers will likely be able to provide you with a program that will help you determine implied volatility, asking you to enter certain factors and then calculating it for you. However, it's only through experience that you'll learn how to spot a stock that's just volatile enough to justify its higher price – again, practice is key.

It's also worth noting that a lot of the risk in options trading comes from volatility, largely because it's impossible to be accurate in your estimates. What happens if an earthquake destroys that company's headquarters? Stocks are going to plummet, and you had absolutely no way to see it coming.

That's why options traders are forced to accept that their fancy formulas are not going to be perfect predictors. They will help, but you should still be conservative in your trading and avoid the temptation to sink everything into a trade you believe could make your fortune thanks to its volatility.

Strategies for a Volatile Market

Long Straddle

This strategy is essentially an amalgamation of the long call and long put trading strategies. You will be using the money options for executing the strategy. You are required to purchase at the money calls along with at the money puts of the same amount. Execute both these transactions simultaneously and ensure that the expiry date for them stays the same. Given that the expiry date is long-term, it gives the underlying security sufficient time to show a price movement and increases your chances of earning a profit. A short-term expiration date doesn't provide much scope for any changes in the price of an asset, so the profitability is also relatively low.

Long Strangle

This is also known as the strangle strategy, and you must place simultaneous orders with your broker. You must purchase calls on relevant security and then by the same number of puts on the security. The options contracts you execute must be out of the money and must be made simultaneously. The best way to go about it is to purchase those securities that are just out of the money instead of ones which are far out of the money. Make sure that the strike prices in both these transactions are equidistant from the existing trading price of the underlying asset.

Strip Straddle

This strategy is quite similar to a long straddle- you will be purchasing at the money calls and at the money puts. The only difference is that the number of puts you purchase will be higher than the calls your purchase. The expiry date and the underlying asset for both these transactions you make will be the same.

The only factor upon which your profitability lies on is the ratio of puts to calls you use. The best ratio is to purchase two puts for every call you make.

Strip Strangle

You stand to earn a profit if the underlying asset makes a big price movement in either direction is. However, your profitability increases if the price movement is downwards instead of upwards. You will be required to purchase out of the money calls and out of the money puts. Ensure that the number of out of the money puts you make are greater than the out of the money calls you to decide to make. So, to begin with, the ratio of 2:1 will work well for you.

Strap Straddle

This is quite similar to the long straddle strategy- you are required to purchase at the money calls along with at the money puts for the same date of expiry. You are required to purchase more calls than ports, and the basic ratio to start with is 2:1. User strategy for certain that there will be an upward movement in the price of the underlying asset instead of a downward price movement.

Strap Strangle

This is quite similar to the Long strangle strategy and uses it when you're quite confident that there will be a dramatic movement in the price of the underlying strategy. You tend to earn a profit if the price moves in either direction, but your profitability increases in the price movement are upward. There are two transactions you must execute- purchase out of the money puts and purchase out of the money calls options. However, the number of out of the money calls you to make must be greater than the out of the money puts. The ratio of out of the money puts out of the money calls must be two to one. So, you will essentially be purchasing twice as many calls as sports.

Long Gut

You are required to purchase in the money call options along with an equal number of in the money put options. All of these will be based on the same underlying security along with the same date of expiration. The decisions you are required to make while using the strategy are related to the strike price you want to use and the date of expiration. It is suggested that to increase your profitability, and reduce the upfront costs, the strike price you must opt for must be closely related to the current trading price of the underlying asset.

Call Ratio Back spread

You are required to purchase calls and right calls to create a call ratio back spread. Since it is a ratio spread, the number of options you execute in each of these transactions will not be the same. As a rule of thumb, try to purchase two calls for every call you write. Always ensure that the total credit for the contracts you've written must be higher than the total debit for the contracts you have acquired.

Put Ratio Back spread

You will earn a profit if the price of the underlying asset moves in either direction; however, your profitability increases if the price of the underlying asset's price goes down instead of going up. You are required to purchase puts and write puts simultaneously. As is obvious, both of these transactions will be based on the same underlying asset. The only difference is that instead of purchasing an equal number of puts, you will be purchasing to puts for every put you right. The puts you purchase must be at the money while the once you write must be in the money. The expiry date, along with the underlying security, must be the same.

Short Calendar Call Spread

The strategy is best used when you are certain that there will be a significant price movement in the value of the underlying security. However, you are uncertain of the direction in which the security will swing. Instead of spending a lot of time trying to analyze the direction of the price change, you can use the strategy. The strategy is likely complicated, and beginners must not attempt it in the first try. There are two transactions you must make. The first transaction is to purchase at the money calls, and the second transaction is to write at the money calls. Since it is a calendar spread, the expiry date is used for both these transactions must be different. The options you decide to purchase must be short-term with a relatively close expiry date while the options you write must be long term with a longer date of expiration.

Short Calendar Put Spread

There are two transactions that are required to execute in this strategy-purchase at the money puts while writing at the money puts. The date of expiration for both these transactions will be different since it is a calendar spread. The price of the contracts that have a longer expiry date will be quite high as compared to the ones with a shorter expiration date. It is based on the basic idea that a substantial movement in the value of the underlying security will mean that the extrinsic value of both the sets of options will end up being equal or close to being full. The initial credit you receive is because of the higher extrinsic value of the options written. So, if the extrinsic value becomes equal on both sites, then that credit which will be created is your profits.

CHAPTER 24:

Price and Patterns

The price of a commodity refers to the cost or rather the value that is attached to it. Price patterns, on the other hand, refer to the formations that appear on a commodity as well as stock charts, which tend to show a certain degree of prediction. One of the essential parts of technical analysis is price patterns. It is worth noting that the easiest way to comprehend about price patterns is by first considering what trade action is. In each day, investors, traders, as well as professionals, let alone institutions are involved in buying and selling of commodities as well the exchange of securities — the numerous types of market participants who buy and sell their products with unique and different reasons. There are also beliefs as well as traditions that surround the art of trading. The aspects create a particular trend that seems predictable hence the development of a pattern.

It is critical to understand that the meeting point of both sellers and buyers for whatever reason is price. In other words, what combines their values as well as their desires is price. The number of commodities, as well as securities in the stock exchange market, tend to differ. Also, the art of seasons tends to affect the pricing of products. The other aspect that affects the pricing of goods and services is the art of supply and demand. In most cases, during a season of a particular product, the supply tends to be high, and the demand in a way tends to reduce. In such situations, the traders are forced to lower the prices of these commodities so as they may attract more buyers. In other words, due to the increased supply, the only aspect worth clearing these goods is that of selling them at a reduced price hence encouraging more buying. On the other hand, when the supply of products and services reduce, what is available in the market tend to decrease. In such season, the demand for such commodities tend to rise, and the traders or rather the sellers take the advantage and hike the prices of these commodities. Thus, the market, as well as the supply of goods and services, plays a critical role in determining the number of products. In other words, they dictate the patterns over which the pricing of commodities takes. The pattern of the price may go for a certain period and can be an excellent basis to forecast price movement in the future. Depending on the rates that are in the market at a given time, you will be in a potion to know whether there will be a price increase or decrease

Price Agreement

It is worth noting that no trading can take place unless there is a good agreement on the pricing of goods and services. In other words, in trade, negotiation is allowed. The aspect is critical in the sense that it will enable the sellers and the buyers to agree on a price that favors both parties. Economics defines demand as the willingness and the ability of clients to buy goods and services at a specific price. Thus, there is a particular art of desire, as well as the knowledge that plays a more prominent role in identifying the best price. Therefore, sellers can't overprice their goods and services for the sake of the customers. Overpricing means that the buyer might be having the willingness to buy some of these goods and services, but the pricing might be too high, and they end up lacking the ability. In such a situation, trade fails to exist as the exchange doesn't occur.

Demand and Supply

What drives the marketing of securities as well the commodities and services in any situation is the demand and supply. In other words, the buyers of any security bring the order in the market while the sellers of these securities bring in the amount of the commodities. It is worth noting that marketing runs continuously throughout the day. In each hour, buyers and sellers compete with each other to get the best price there is. In other words, the buyers keep looking for sellers who are relatively cheap and own quality goods and promising securities. The buyers will also consider checking the marketing trends on these commodities or instead of securities before they deliberate on paying for them.

As indicated in the graph above, when the price is low, the demand for the shares tend to be high. For instance, when the price is $100, the demand tends to range at 600. The aspect indicates that the more the price is high, the low demand is expected. In that when the price hikes to $400, the demand reduces to around 300.

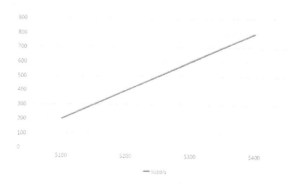

On the other hand, an increase in price encourages the suppliers to supply more. Thus, when the price is about $100, the supply is relatively low and stands at 200. However, when the price shoots to $400. The supply also increases to about 600. The aspect is critical in the sense that it allows the trader to measure the price in the market before supplying more.

Equilibrium

In a hypothetical situation, the purpose of negotiation and agreement brings the two parties in a common ground and allows them to agree. If a buyer is willing to buy several shares from a particular organization, it is the role of the seller to convince the buyer on the need to acquire such shares. The aspect is critical in the sense that it allows the buyer to have a reason for agreeing with a specific price. There are cases where buyers, on the other hand, take part in convincing sellers the need to reduce their pricing. The aspect brings some sense of harmony that tends to make trading more enjoyable. It is worth noting that the sellers also have limitations that help them sell goods and services here and there. For instance, if an individual seller is limited to the selling if 4 million shares in a day, and then a buyer brings in a proposal of buying more than 4 million shares, it is the role of the seller to distribute the demand in several days. The aspect ensures that even other buyers that might be willing to buy shares from the same organization get a taste of them on the same day. It is also crucial for buyers to avoid such a scenario. The aspect is linked to the fact that when one buys a huge or a bulk number of shares, the chances are that the supply tends to reduce, and the price shoots for no apparent reason. The aspect may lead to loss of funds when the shares are either priced at a low price.

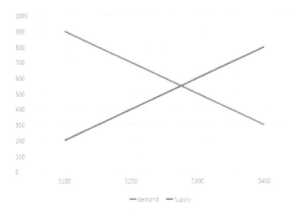

As shown above, an equilibrium is arrived at when the supply of shares is the same as the demand of the shares. In other words, at a price of $550, the demand and the supply are said to be at equilibrium. At this point, the pricing tends to be similar in all situations and no added advantage over buying shares or rather shares from a certain organization. The aspect is due to the fact that all the shares are similar, and their supply tends to be similar.

The main objective of getting the best price is to ensure that the purchasing of shares is effective. The aspect is linked to the fact that even after buying a massive number of shares, there comes a time when such shares ought to be resold for one to earn profits. If the pricing of these shares is relatively lower than the initial price, it means that the buyer who had a considerable number of shares will have to accept and suffer a huge loss. Thus, the pricing of these shares is defined by several aspects.

The nature of the shares also determines its pricing. In other words, the behaviors of the shares in terms of how they behave in the market also determines their pricing. For instance, there are some of the stocks that tend to be more aggressive than others. In most cases, such shares maintain a high price despite the level of competition. Such shares may encourage one to buy a large number of shares. However, it is, at times challenging to predict the pricing of such shares. The aspect is linked to the fact that their stability tends to be affected by issues of demand and supply. In other words, if the demand increases, the balance of the shares may cause the seller to hike their prices.

In most cases, the buyers tend to shy off, and the demand tends to reduce. In most cases, when the order lowers, the sellers are forced to reduce the procuring of these shares. The aspect means that those buyers who had purchased the shares at a higher price will be forced to resell them at a low price hence making loses. In most cases, when the prices of stocks start to reduce, the aspect causes all the owners of such shares to resell them with the fear that the price may keep reducing.

The process of buying and selling of shares keeps shifting from time to time. The pricing keeps changing until an equilibrium is arrived at. In most cases, the balance is reached when the demand for shares is equal to the supply of shares as well. The aspect is critical in the sense that it allows the buyers and the sellers to agree on the best price that favors all of them. Although such hypothetical situations don't last for long. Over time, the pricing comes to a level where those willing to buy gates the ability to do so. In other cases, the buyers and the sellers go into a situation where they are aggressive over being satisfied by a specific price. With time, the parties agree, and the pricing gets a pattern that tends to be predictable over a specified period.

It is worth noting that companies own these shares. The aspect indicates that when the organizations or rather the premises do well in terms of making huge profits, it's worth tends to rise hence the pricing of the shares. In the same cases, when it makes loses, its net worth tends to lower hence the reduction in price. However, in most organizations, the drops, as well as the profits on the premises, tend to be seasonal. Thus, analysts able to identify the period over which these prices reduce or hike. Therefore, one can do the right timing and amass a considerable profit in the long run.

Continuation and Reversal Price Patterns

Large institutions are the ones who are responsible for taking particular views as well as drive the prices daily. They may go to the extent of driving the prices for weeks and sometimes for months. They make sure that they will attract all the buyers and sellers. After they get all of them, they will take them to a certain level and make sure that they transact and help them take positions. When they are making the transaction, they will interact in the process, and that will enhance a good relationship promoting business. In such interactions is where they will discuss the suitable prices to put on certain products. When there is an agreement on the costs to rule in the market.

CHAPTER 25:

What Every Investor Should Do

Understand Market Basics

In the modern world, investment has been made accessible to the average person. Most employers who offer retirement savings plans often sponsor an education day, so employees can gain some familiarity with the types of retirement plans and options that are available to them. In addition, with the proliferation of cable news networks, specialized programming, the internet, and social media, there is no shortage of information widely available to virtually anyone, anywhere.

Especially in the information age, knowledge is power. Before you jump right into trading on the options market, take some time to familiarize yourself with the basics of market dynamics. Options traders use a language that is unique to their niche in the investment world, and many outsiders may be completely perplexed and unable to understand much of what they say. In addition, the ability to tolerate a certain amount of financial risk is an inseparable component of successful investing.

Play by the Rules

As an options trader, you will be in competition with other traders and investors. Much of your success in investing--including making valuable connections in the investment world--will result from your ability to play by the rules. The stock market is a living thing, and the activity of traders has a huge impact on its health and volatility. We are all tempted to be maverick investors who leave a legacy of innovation, but understanding the fundamentals will work in your favor.

Specifically, option prices increase or decrease as a result of changes in share prices and volatility.

So, when share prices increase, call options make money and put options lose money; when share prices decrease, put options make money and call options lose money. Options also move in relation to volatility; when share prices are stable, greater volatility can increase the options pricing. So, when volatility increases, buying options makes money; when volatility decreases, selling options makes money.

Understanding these four basic rules can help you become a better trader.

Adapt Your Strategy to Market Conditions

Once you're up and running in the world of professional options trading, you will gain confidence as you see your efforts pay off in returns to your options account. As you move from a Level 1 trading account to a Level 2 trading account, you will likely develop a preference for a certain type of options trades—maybe covered calls or married puts. Familiarity with the language and mechanics of the options trading profession is definitely something that will work in your favor. However, it is important to remember that as you move up the ladder, you will gain access to a wider array of trading tools and strategies. As you gain knowledge and experience, remember that no matter how comfortable you have become with a select number of options trading strategies, there will always be additional aspects of nuance that can enhance your skill as a trader and increase the profitability of your efforts. The key to ensuring success is not just in choosing the best strategy in relation to the performance of the underlying asset. You must also consider the overall market conditions and whether those conditions may have an effect on the future performance of that asset. Although one strategy may have worked in the past under similar conditions, considering changes in current conditions will help you adjust your strategy to ensure you continue to build on your past success.

Always Have an Exit Plan

Picking a stock, formulating an options strategy to generate income from the stock's performance, and then contacting your broker to initiate an opening transaction is a good beginning. But this plan is not a complete strategy. The most important part of any options strategy is not how to get in—it's how to get out.

The payoff of an options strategy may result from buying the underlying stock at below market value, from accepting a cash settlement deposit for a put option on stock with declining value, or even from profiting from an increase in the cost of the options premium by selling the contract before it expires.

However, you believe the asset you have identified may provide you with an opportunity to construct a profitable options trading strategy, conjecture and hope should not be part of that strategy. Before you complete an opening transaction, make sure you are very clear about your specific goal for entering the contract. After you complete the opening transaction, you will be faced with one of three possible outcomes:

1. The market and the target stocks moved in the direction you predicted.

2. The market or the target stocks move in a direction you did not predict, resulting in unexpected losses.

3. The market or the target stocks move in a direction you did not predict, resulting in unexpected gains.

Similarly, you should have three responses ready for each of these developments:

1. If you are faced with the first result, you should have an exit strategy already prepared. Whatever else is happening around you, as long as your assets are on the right track, do not deviate from your plan.

2. If there are unexpected changes that are not favorable to your position on the underlying asset, what plan did you formulate to exit the contract so you can minimize your losses?

3. If there are unexpected changes that are favorable to your position on the underlying asset, what plan did you formulate to exit the contract so you can capitalize on these gains?

No matter what happens, make sure you can answer all 3 questions before you enter an options contract. Then, once you have laid the groundwork for a successful options trade, stick with your plan, even if you think you could make a few more dollars by improvising.

What Every Investor Should Avoid

Doubling up to Cover Losses

"Doubling up" is a prime example of how an options trader may ignore his original exit strategy if the market or the underlying stocks fail to perform the way he had expected when he originally constructed his strategy.

For example, let's say a trader buys a call option for 100 shares of Company B, with a strike price of $45. At the time he purchased the call option, Company B was trading at $44. The trader expects the share price to rise to $47 before the contract expires. Immediately after the opening transaction, though, the stock price slips to $43.

The premium for a call option with a strike price of $45 is further out-of-the-money now than at opening, In addition, there's still plenty of time before expiration. As a result, to compensate for any potential losses if the stock rises to only $46, the trader may be tempted to "double up" by buying another $45 call option at the reduced premium price.

If this trader were only purchasing stocks, he may have celebrated the unexpected drop in share value and immediately purchased as many additional shares as possible, with a goal of greater long-term return. But options trading works differently. The options trader is focused on short-term returns, and if the stock price fails to put the contract in-the-money by the expiration date, the trader loses on not only one contract, but two.

The smart trader will remember that he created an exit plan for this scenario and will stick with it. Though it may be tempting to purchase an additional call option, he should judge the wisdom of such a purchase by asking himself if he would buy the second call option if he were not already in the middle of a trade. If this is not ordinarily a contract he would enter into--and it isn't, because that was definitely not his strategy in his opening transaction--then market conditions and stock performance that defy expectations are probably the worst reasons for him to change that view.

Instead, he should either stay in his contract to see if the stock eventually rebounds and makes the contract profitable, or sell the contract immediately, cut his losses, and look for another opportunity that makes more sense.

Trying to Hit a "Home Run" Every Time

Popular culture portrays Wall Street as a sort of heaven for adrenaline junkies, in which highly skilled traders spend their days chasing down successively bigger, sexier, and more lucrative deals. The only barriers for these imaginary gods of the stock market appear to be failing to out-trade and outperform all their friends and colleagues and thereby missing out on bragging rights at the local pub at the end of the trading day.

A skilled options trader can make huge gains using well-planned strategies. Certainly, this should be a goal for every options trader, but it is a difficult goal to achieve for many reasons.

First, the perfect storm of daily skyrocketing corporate share prices hardly ever occurs. Most stocks maintain stability and change very little from day to day, so the paradigmatic conditions for a highly profitable options contract are hard to come by. As a result, if your approach to options trading strategies consists of trying to arrange contracts that guarantee payouts that are not likely to occur, or to approach market analysis from a perspective that a lesser degree of volatility is the exception rather than the rule, you will be missing the considerable opportunities the options trading market presents for disciplined investors.

Markets and indexes may not make dramatic swings very often, and that's probably a good thing.

However, markets do consistently move by several points in both directions each day. By studying market behavior, you will have a better grasp of what types of changes are likely to occur and when.

Using this knowledge to buy and sell options contracts that conform to sound market fundamentals can help you earn steady weekly returns. Practiced correctly, a well-disciplined approach to options trading can provide any skilled investor with the opportunity to create a source of steady residual income to enhance an existing portfolio.

Buying Cheap Options

An options contract that is very far out-of-the-money will likely have a comparatively low premium. For example, let's say Company ABC is trading at $30.00 per share. Your broker tells you the share price is likely to increase and that there is a call option on this company with a strike price of $32.00 for a premium of $3.25.

You find another call option for the same company with a strike price of $35.00 and a premium of only $1.10. You know the share price is going to increase, and the call option with the lower premium would result in a larger profit, but there's a reason for that--the lower premium results from the fact that the share price is not likely to reach $35.00 by the expiration date. These types of options are traps for beginning traders, so avoid them whenever you can.

Investing in Illiquid Options

The last time you prepared your company's balance sheet, filed your taxes, or appraised your investment portfolio, you may have considered your "liquid assets" as part of the calculation of your total assets. Your liquid assets are those assets—such as cars and trucks, office equipment, or real estate—that can quickly be converted into cash by selling them.

CHAPTER 26:

How to Choose the Right Strategy?

Before you can start trading, you must understand your reasons for trading, find the right broker, discover the opportunities to trade, and come up with a trading plan. One of the most important steps, while making a trade is to decide when to enter and the position to assume. You might probably have all the information you need about options, but it will not do you much good unless you start using that information to make the right decisions to improve your overall finances. Perhaps the most challenging part of planning every trade you make is to select a strategy you use. This stands true, especially if you're just getting started with options trading. At times, even experienced traders tend to struggle with all this. So, don't worry if you are a little confused right now. Once you go through the information given in this manuscript, you will be in a better position to make smart financial decisions.

Important Aspects

When it comes to the perfect strategy for trading in options, there are five various aspects you must consider, and they are as follows.

Your outlook

Your outlook about an option primarily refers to what you expect from the underlying security. Your perspective is about whether you expect a rise or fall in the price of the underlying security in the future. In various forms of investing, these are the only two outlooks that are profitable. For instance, a stock trader can purchase talks that he expects will increase in value or short sell such stocks which he thinks will decrease in value. These are the only ways in which he can on a profit. However, when it comes to trading in options, there are four potential outlooks, and they are an expectation that the market will be bullish, bearish, neutral, or volatile. This certainly means there is a lot to think about, but it also increases the chances of your profitability. The four market conditions to be mindful of are.

- Bullish- expecting the price to increase

- Bearish- expecting the price the decrease

- Neutral- price will stay relatively stable

- Volatile- price can significantly sway either way.

Your outlook can be made more specific. For instance, your outlook can be significantly bullish or even moderately bullish. By making this outlook as precise as possible, you are making it easier to select the right strategy for investing. For instance, if you're expecting that the price of the underlying security will experience a significant increase in its price, you will not opt for a strategy, which generates profits based on small movements in the price. Given the various plans available, you are also free to combine your outlook. For instance, you might expect the price of an underlying security to stay neutral in the short-term and increase significantly in the long run. There are strategies that can be used to help you earn a profit by combining these outlooks. This just goes on to prove the flexibility offered by options.

The risk involved

When it comes to investing, there's always a certain degree of risk involved. There are some strategies, which have to reduce your risk, whereas others are quite risky. According to your risk profile, and you must opt for a specific approach. Apart from this, you must also consider the risk to reward ratio. It's a general belief that the higher the risk involved, the greater the reward you can receive. So, take some time and calculate the total risk you can easily sustain without denting your finances.

Once you have this number, it becomes easier to select a strategy. Also, never invest more than you can stand to lose. This is a cardinal rule of investing you must never overlook.

Single position versus options spread

Options trading usually works on the creation of various spreads. It essentially means the combination of multiple positions you must assume to enter an overall position. By using spreads, you can effectively reduce the risk associated with investing in options along with the cost of investment. It's always better to use sprites instead of a single position. By entering a single position, you are essentially buying a writing only one specific type of options contract. The advantages of this technique are that the number of transactions involved and less; therefore, the commission payable on each trade will certainly be less when compared to options spread. If you are interested in only making small trades initially, then a single position is quite profitable. Therefore, whether you opt for a single position or options spread will depend on the occasion and the market conditions.

Amount of trading involves

For becoming an options trader, you must create a trading account with a broker. Usually, these accounts are assigned a specific trading limit. These limits help protect their customers from assuming risks higher than what they can stand and also for certain regulatory purposes. If the trading level is quite low, then there are only a few trading strategies you can use. So, the trading level helps determine your overall investment and trading strategies you use.

The complexity of the strategy

There are certain trading strategies that are quite simple, and then there are those that are a little complex. Some strategies only involve dealing in one or two transactions, whereas others combine several transactions. So, the complexity involved also influences the strategy you opt for. An important aspect for determining the potential profit or loss you incur depends on your entry and exit points. If there are multiple transactions and assets involved, it becomes slightly complex. As you go through the various strategies deliberated in this manuscript, you will realize there are certain strategies that are quite easy to understand others which will take some practice. If you don't understand a strategy initially, don't attempt it. Once you gain the confidence required and have been trading for some time, you can attempt any of the complex strategies. After all, the idea is to maximize your earnings.

CHAPTER 27:

How to Be A Thriving Option Investor

1) Have your trading style. The intended trading style is usually used in the trading plan. Your trading style should be strictly followed and updated with new skills and information as you engage in various options transactions. Follow the program without any other impact and watch how you grow by trading options.

2) Trading plan. Unplanned planning for failure. This means that the loser will only be reflected if no planning occurs. Successful entrepreneurs have big plans. Great ideas include the right strategies, features, discussions, in-depth research, great self-discipline, goals, and reasonable goals. Establishing good trading plans is a clear reflection of the great success in options trading.

3) Emotionally stable. Emotions can be very distracting when we get involved in various aspects of our lives. Losing trade should be treated as a bad day, which is useful with good educational experience and knowledge for a bright future. Winning days should also be a learning day, appreciating the right moves expressed that day.

4) Intensive learning and proactivity. Life always remains stagnant when you stop learning. Knowledge is good and evil, including master and learn every possible expressed move

5) In options trading and be very interested in choosing moral essence from earlier episodes and squeezing out all goodness from it. Also, subscribe to a variety of channels and blogs to get the extensive knowledge you need in trading options.

Learning allows you to inform and educate about actual trading activities that are usually involved in options trading.

6) Secure, accurate business records. Try to learn from your mistakes, although sometimes it can be difficult to make simple decisions based on your earlier results because option trading is a matter of happy and sad seasons, governed by several established strategies that have been correctly defined in the options trading plan. We encourage you to learn from past mistakes and strategic development to become a successful options investor.

7) Determination and commitment. This entails a lot of thrusts that should rule a beginner or an experienced trader to get what is best for him in options trading and getting down learn some tips on how to succeed as an options trader.

8) Be flexible. Another thing to add is that when you feel it, the market does not suit you at all during this particular period of options trading, find something constructive to do. Master every possible market move that will likely occur in options trading and master it.

9) Basic understanding and interpretation. The trader should be familiar with the necessary market terminology to understand the primary activities of the market and learn the different ways to start and handle options trading. The interpretation consists in the analysis of actual commercial transactions on the market and obtaining the necessary information in each of the commercial activities. This helps the investor always pay attention to reality

10) Market, not hype, depending on significant market terms.

11) Be aggressive. Being aggressive in options trading means that there is a desire for great success, and the chances of getting big profits are so high. A dynamic option trader most often

participates in in-depth scientific research, learning new and learning new lucrative trade moves. This gives the trader extensive experience and skills to face all kinds of risks that may be involved in the market, and in a short time, the trader accredited a great expert in options trading.

12) Emotionally stable. Different feelings on the market should not control an investor engaged in options trading. Lost days should not in any way discourage the trader from deciding to stay with the market hype. It is recommended that investors follow their plan and always stick to it down their different strategies.

13) Excellent choice of goods. The option trader must select the appropriate sell option.

14) Weigh are you able to handle the right inventory and manage the necessary risks that are highly involved in them? Most importantly, will the shares benefit the investor in making large profits?

15) Good capital management. When money is important this comes to trade. Monitor and plan any amount of capital that you plan to use on the market. Always be careful with the amount of money you put into each option. Accepting losses is still an alternative when it comes to options trading, a failure that can knock you down and lead you to bankruptcy. Plan the capital that you plan to invest in the company.

16) Powerful trading platforms. The platform on which various commercial activities take place is essential in all types of involvement in option transactions. Your best platform should consist of fantastic navigation tools, learning sources, and other amazing features.

17) Selling options are most often preferred than buying options while practicing buying and selling strategies that ultimately help the investor to make a large amount of profit.

18) Correct time. As an entrepreneur, you should be informed about good and bad times. Enter the market when the time is quite favorable. Bad timing leads to significant losses in the options trading market, which leads to a substantial decline in finance. Bad timing leads to significant losses in the options trading market, which leads to a significant decrease in funding that eventually causes bankruptcy.

Strategies that are successful in options trading

1) Good strategies set out in the options trading plan should be a priority. Back-testing, measuring, and weighing current strategies by comparing them with some earlier historical records and learning about growth and events that have occurred in recent periods is highly recommended by experts.

2) Use the appropriate period. A longer period, for example, five years is recommended during in-depth research and analysis of various sources to establish good strategies. Remember to choose a fairly long period to get up-to-date information and to report it as part of learning.

3) Covered connection. This type of strategy includes both trading in underlying shares and options contracts. The ultimate goal of a secured connection is to collect income through premiums and mainly sell inventory that you already own. Here are some ways to consider when creating a program connection:

4) Buy shares and buy in the form of shares. Sell a purchase contract for every 100 shares you own. Then wait for the connection to be made.

5) The risk associated with secured connections maintains a cautious inventory position that may fail over time. Large parts of the profits from this particular combination are equal to the price of the specified call option and the lower purchase price of the underlying shares.

6) We are introducing to the market. This strategy consists in the fact that the investor has made two purchases on the stock exchange and a put option. The advantage of this is that as an options investor, you can protect yourself against several losses. Launching is also considered beneficial when buying a security that has an optimistic attitude. The market launch strategy is also necessary to protect the depreciation, in particular of share prices.

7) Market sales are also called the synthetic long call because of the similarities in the number of potential profits on both sides.

8) Spread options. This strategy was established by selling several options and purchase options of the same class and from the same collateral with different exercise prices and expiry dates.

9) Butterfly spread. Butterfly includes four calls to buy and sell and is also considered a market-neutral strategy that can pay the majority of its underlying shares without worrying about expiration dates.

10) There are several varieties of butterfly spreads that usually use four types of options with three different strike prices. To add, different types of butterflies have different levels of maximum profit amount and maximum loss amount, which usually occur when trading options.

11) The strategy of short proportions of bulls. The short bull ratio strategy is used to benefit from profits obtained due to increased trading safety.

12) The market in a similar way as we usually buy connections in a given period.

13) The spread of the bull condor. This is a type of strategy that aims to return a profit if the actual price of the security paper decides to raise to the expected price range during a certain

trading period, affecting the large profits achieved for the options trader and the limited number of risks.

14) Place a strategy for spreading the pointer. This strategy involves the purchase of several put options and the purchase of more put options with different exercise prices and the same underlying shares over a given period.

15) Timing belt strategy. The Straddle strategy uses one buy and two calls with a similar strike price with the same expiration date and the underlying shares that are usually stagnant during a given trading period. The investor applies this type of strategy in the hope of obtaining higher profits compared to the usual straddle strategy in a given trading period.

16) A long cart. This is also known as buying a coupon, which mainly involves buying options to buy and buy similar underlying shares and keeping the same striking price and equal timelines that were involved when trading options. Long-term options are usually associated with unlimited profits with limited risk management options that are implemented when the options trader feels worse due to market volatility rates.

17) Choke. Commonly called by strangling, it is buying small options from similar underlying shares and having equal amounts due.

18) Dates in the same period. Long suffocation is also associated with large chunks of profit and benefit, and during actual trading is likely to involve less risk.

19) Bear put a spread strategy. This type of strategy is to buy options in the belief that it will benefit from the expected decline that is expected to affect the underlying inventory and to extract another package with the same expiration date and a much lower strike price to cover some of the costs that it had experienced.

20) Strategic protective collar. This type of option strategy protects the trader from such large losses, but at the same time limits the trader from obtaining large profits and benefits. An investor initiates a collar by buying a put option and the same every minute when initiating a put option.

21) Bull spread. This is a type of options trading strategy that is appropriate to benefit from an increase in the actual share price. There are usually two buy options, and the range between the highest strike price and the lowest is set.

22) She secured naked cash. This type of strategy involves writing for money or out of money and putting away a certain amount of cash to buy shares.

Glossary

L isted options: A listed option is an option that qualifies for trading at a national trading platform like the Chicago Board Options Exchange, CBOE. A listed option generally represents 100 shares of a particular stock. Such an option with 100 shares is also referred to as 1 contract. Each contract has fixed expiration dates and strike prices.

The price, or total cost, of any option is referred to as the premium. It is affected by a number of factors including volatility, time value, strike price, and stock price.

Contract names: Options contracts do have names or options symbols similar to ticker symbols for stocks.

Ask price: This is the asking price that a seller will accept to trade the option. Basically, should you wish to purchase options, then this would be the premium that you would pay.

Volume: This refers to the total number of contracts that get traded in one day

Change: This refers to the difference in price from the earlier to the current trading period. Sometimes change is expressed in terms of percentage.

Volatility: Volatility is simply the measure of a stock's price swing measured between the low and high prices of each day. For a long time, volatility has been measured using past data.

IV, also known as implied volatility, measures the likelihood that a market considers a stock will experience significant price swing. There are certain tools that are used to measure some of these parameters. One of these is Vega. Vega is a pricing model that calculates the theoretical effect of a single point change in implied volatility.

When the implied volatility is high, it means options prices will be high due to the potential upside for the options contract. It is good to keep in mind that volatility measurements are only estimates and never accurate. They are mostly predictions on the expected change of an option's price.

Employee stock option: While these are not readily available for all traders, they are a type of call option. Plenty of listed companies offer stock options to their treasured and talented staff members, especially management, in order to retain them for a long period of time.

Employee stock options are very similar to ordinary stock options as a holder receives the right, but not obligation, to purchase stocks at a certain price and within a stipulated time period. However, the contract only exists between the company owners or board and an employee. Others cannot trade or exchange it at the options stock markets.

This is different however if the options are listed. A listed option represents a contract between two different parties. This contract is completely unrelated to the company and easily be traded at the markets.

Terms Describing an Option's Value

We do not describe an option's performance as up, down, or level. This kind of description is not sufficient. Instead, we can definite performance in one of three distinct ways.

Essentially, it is beneficial to the call option owner when the stock price is greater than the strike price. On the other hand, a put option is said to be in the money when the price of the stock is less than the strike price.

Out of the money: An option is said to be out of the money when there is absolutely no monetary gain expected in exercising it. This means it is a lot less lucrative or financially viable to sell stocks and shares at the strike price than it would in the general securities market. Therefore, we say that a call option is out of the money is the strike price is higher than the stock price. A put option, on the other hand, is said to be out of the money anytime that the stock price is high than the strike price.

At the money: Sometimes the strike price is just about equal to the stock price. In such a situation, we say that the option is at the money.

Options Seller and Buyer Terms

There are special terms used to refer to options traders. In other situations, we'd refer to the traders as buyers and sellers. However, when it comes to options trading, a more technical term is used.

Writer: The term writer refers to an investor who holds an options contract and is selling it. When the writer sells the option, they will receive a premium from the buyer. The buyer will be buying the right to buy a specific number of shares at a strike price.

Holder: A holder is basically an investor seeking to purchase an options contract. A call options holder will buy an options contract and gain the right to purchase the underlying stock under stipulated terms. A put holder possesses all the rights to sell the underlying stock.

A holder and a writer are generally on opposite sides of an options transaction. One writes an option while the other signs up to it. However, the main difference between these two is the kind of losses they are exposed to.

Conclusion

Thank you for taking the time to read this manuscript and finish it all the way to the end! I hope that you have found it to be informative and educational. Options are an exciting way to get into trading, and the potential is there to make quick profits! To any beginner, things may be a bit too complex with all the jargon that is involved, however, take the time to learn and understand what each concept means and soon things will be much easier. Also, you are here for one purpose, to know how to trade with options and earn profits!

Hopefully, you will take the lessons at heart to mitigate your risks and trade carefully. The first principle to follow in this regard is only to put as much money as you can afford to lose into the stock market. That way, in the event of total loss, you would still be able to go ahead and carry on with your life, and possibly raise more money later to try again.

There are numerous ways of creating wealth but trading the markets is among the most popular. Trading is known to generate high returns whether it is active or passive. The most lucrative form of trading involves trading options. Any trader that wants to grow their wealth should move away from traditional investments and move to more lucrative stock market instruments. For instance, traders should invest their funds in options to grow wealth much faster and in significant amounts.

You can buy and sell options at the markets just like you do with other securities like shares and so on. Only that options are derivates and therefore they are traded a little differently than other securities. Derivatives obtain their value from an underlying or other asset. This asset can be a stock, shares, commodities, currencies, and so on. As the price of the underlying asset rises and falls, that of the option is also affected.

When it comes to trading the markets, we know that we are supposed to buy when prices are low and then sell when prices are high. This is simple enough to understand. However, options trading is not necessarily that simple. It is a little more complex in comparison. If you take time to understand the underlying principles and how different strategies work, then you will get a better understanding of options.

Options do carry a higher than average risk because of various factors. They are known to be risky and complicated with some traders losing all their money and in some cases exposure to unlimited losses. However, these risks become a threat when you do not properly understand how options work and how to trade in them. If you learn the right way and take the time to learn all about them, then options should be pretty easy to understand and much less complicated.

The fact is that options traders assume much larger risks than the ordinary trader. There are a couple of factors that come to play when dealing options. These include time decay and implied volatility. Time decay is crucial because all options contracts are time-bound. A contract loses its value with time. It has premium value once it is written and sold. From there onwards, the value will keep depreciating.

Different traders use options for various purposes. There are those who use options to hedge against risks. Others use options to protect against future price hikes. However, the majority of options traders are in it to make huge profits which are possible using this strategy.

Made in the USA
Monee, IL
02 December 2020